VISIBLE MENDING FOR
THE CLOTHES YOU LOVE

WELL WORN

ilex

SKYE PENNANT

First published in Great Britain in 2024 by Ilex, an imprint of
Octopus Publishing Group Ltd
Carmelite House
50 Victoria Embankment
London EC4Y 0DZ
www.octopusbooks.co.uk

An Hachette UK Company
www.hachette.co.uk

The authorized representative in the EEA is Hachette Ireland
8 Castlecourt Centre, Dublin 15, D15 XTP3, Ireland (email: info@hbgi.ie)

Text copyright ©
Skye Pennant 2024
Design and layout copyright ©
Octopus Publishing Group Ltd 2024

8 above: Takayuki Fuchigami/Associated Press/Alamy Stock Photo

All rights reserved. No part of this work may be reproduced or utilized in any form or by any means, electronic or mechanical, including photocopying, recording or by any information storage and retrieval system, without the prior written permission of the publisher.

Skye Pennant has asserted her right under the Copyright, Designs and Patents Act 1988 to be identified as the author of this work.

ISBN 978-1-78157-922-0
eISBN 978-1-78157-923-7

A CIP catalogue record for this book is available from the British Library.

Printed and bound in China

10 9 8 7 6 5 4 3 2

Publisher: Alison Starling
Commissioning Editor: Ellie Corbett
Managing Editor: Rachel Silverlight
Project Editor: Faye Robson
Editorial Assistant: Ellen Sleath
Art Director: Ben Gardiner
Photography: Kim Lightbody
Prop Stylist: Rachel Vere
Illustrations: Caitlin Keegan
Production Manager: Caroline Alberti

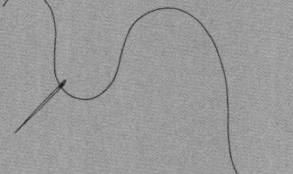

Contents

Introduction — 5

Sustainability: why mend clothes? — 9
How to use this book — 12
Understanding fabrics — 15
Needles — 19
Threads — 20
Other supplies — 22
Introduction to darning — 24
Introduction to sashiko — 28
Introduction to patching — 33
Starting & finishing your repair — 34
Troubleshooting: problems to look out for — 36
Caring for your repairs — 39
When not to mend: a note before we begin — 40

1. *Jeans* — 43
2. *Jumpers & knitwear* — 63
3. *Shirts* — 85
4. *T-shirts* — 99
5. *Leggings* — 111
6. *Socks* — 121
7. *Jackets* — 131
8. *Delicate fabrics* — 141

Further reading & acknowledgements — 144

Introduction

In 2019 I was living in Brighton, England and working as a textiles technician in a high school. It was a job that introduced me to teaching in a way that I had never considered before – being an introvert, the idea of standing at the front of a room and addressing a whole class terrified me! But the kids were amazing, and I absolutely loved sharing sewing and textiles knowledge with them individually, from the sidelines. This was also the year that, while browsing vintage shops with my sister, I found a Speedweve darning loom hidden away in a glass cabinet, boxed and in perfect working order. Having always had a penchant for traditional sewing tools (scissors, thimbles, thread unpickers and the like), I was over the moon. But at that point I had no idea that these two events would be the start of my visible mending journey.

I've always repaired clothing invisibly where I could – taking up hems, fixing buttons, covering up holes – but visible mending opened up a whole new creative avenue. I studied fashion design at university, and have since spent over 15 years working with textiles in one way or another: I'm constantly fascinated by the lifespan of all forms of textiles. From the initial design sketches through to the cloth production, then on to the pattern cutters and garment workers who bring the clothing to life, there is a whole story woven through our clothing before we've even started wearing it. Although my love of textiles never wavered, I struggled with the industry, and it was during my time at university that I began to learn about the huge environmental impact of mass-market clothing production, as well as the horrifying truth about some garment workers and the abuses they endure. It took a long time for me to find a space in which I felt able to continue working with textiles in a way that reflected my values. Slow stitch club became that space.

Slow stitch club took shape during 2020 when I started putting together a kit and designing tools to help people get started with visible mending. Instagram became a gallery for me to post the repairs I was creating, as well as sharing the truths I was learning about fast fashion, along with – as it turns out – many other people in the online visible mending community. I also began teaching workshops online (after just one in-person workshop in March, before the COVID lockdown) to small groups of people all over the world who wanted to learn how to start repairing their clothes. In the years since, I've set up an online shop selling my kits and tools, and continue to run workshops. I take on repair commissions for those who aren't able to do the mending themselves, and have also worked with brands like TOAST and The Seam to help promote the importance of clothing repair.

I really believe that our favourite pieces of clothing can become a wearable scrapbook for us. The wear and tear our clothing collects tells a story of the lives we have lived in them, and will always be unique to us. I think it's an amazing act to take the time and skills to mend our clothes, and this act is as integral to the life of a garment as the weaving of the cloth or the construction of the seams. Mending techniques such as patching and darning can be seen throughout history, whether it was done at a time when fabric was valued as a currency in its own right, or out of necessity due to poverty or wartime scarcity.

Visible mending takes traditional techniques such as patching, darning and sashiko to repair clothing in an intentionally visible and creative way. It flips the idea of repair on its head by taking what was once a skill judged by how invisible a repair could be and turning it into a celebration of the stitches and skills required to give clothing a new lease of life. It also allows us the time and space to slow down and express our creativity in a joyful way that not only rejects perfectionism, but also makes a political statement against fast fashion.

Another thing I love about visible mending is that you can never 'complete' it or finish learning. Every single piece of clothing will present a new kind of damage or require a specific kind of repair technique. I find it inspiring that this means that every repair presents its own challenge, and the chance to hone the techniques you most love to do.

My hope is that this book can act as a compendium for visible clothing repair, one that you'll return to time and time again, no matter the item of clothing or the area of damage. I want it to inspire you to look at your clothes differently, and to feel excited to try your hand at creating your own tactile and wearable scrapbook: a collection of stitches on the clothes you love that tells your stories, changes the way we view damage, reclaims traditional craft skills, and allows you the time and space to slow down and feel encouraged and supported to live a more sustainable life.

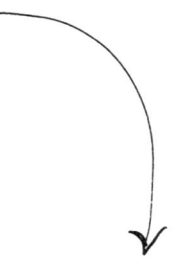

Our favourite pieces of clothing can become a wearable scrapbook for us.

The fashion industry is one of the top most polluting industries on the planet.

Sustainability: why mend clothes?

The environmental impact of clothing

The fashion industry is one of the top most polluting industries on the planet. Overconsumption has become the norm, which means the value we attach to our clothing is diminishing. Clothes are staying in our wardrobes for less time and, due to the rapidity of trend cycles and reduction in clothing costs, they are not considered to be worth repairing. In 2022, fast fashion brand Pretty Little Thing was selling clothing for as little as 8 UK pence (approx. 10 US cents) on Black Friday – a shockingly low cost that promotes the attitude that clothing is disposable.[1] It's important to question here what the garment makers were paid for their work if the retail price was so little, as well as considering the conditions and working environments that would have been necessitated by the production of this clothing. Alongside them, online retailer Shein has been said to churn out an unbelievable 10,000 new products a day, while their website features a countdown clock which creates a false sense of urgency about the clothing available to buy at a particular price and encourages excessive purchasing.[2] An increase in the production of synthetic fibres and fabrics also means that the clothing being discarded is often not recyclable and heads straight to landfill.

In a blog post from July 2022, the environmental news organization Earth.org found that since the year 2000, clothing sales have doubled from 100 to 200 billion units a year, but the average number of times that an item of clothing is worn has decreased by 36 percent overall.[3] The charity Clothes Aid states on their website that Britons send 700,000 tonnes (700,000 US tons) of clothing to recycling centres, textile banks, clothes collections and to charities each year, which is enough to fill 459 Olympic-size swimming pools.[4]

The repercussions of this on the environment can be seen from the diminishing Aral Sea in central Asia through to the clothing mountains in Chile's Atacama desert (see opposite, above). There is also a huge amount to unpack here in regard to the overconsumption of fashion in the Western world and how this is affecting Indigenous areas and cultures that have been dumped – quite literally – with the problem. This book aims to share the skills and techniques you need to get started in repairing your favourite clothes, based on my experience of textiles, but I really recommend learning more about these issues from those who can share their stories and knowledge. I've put together a short reading (and listening!) list at the back of the book (see page 144), which I hope you'll find helpful in giving this important subject more context.

The importance of mending

The term 'climate anxiety' has become all too familiar in the last few years. It can feel overwhelming to know what to do when large companies wield so much power, yet so little is being done to help combat the huge climate issues we face. Although I have, on occasion, been told that my efforts to repair clothing right down to my socks won't make a difference, the act of mending in itself has become a therapy to help me find my place, and I have repeatedly heard this from people attending my workshops too.

In Autumn 2021, the Waste and Resources Action Plan (WRAP.ngo) released their latest report: 'Clothing longevity and circular business models receptivity in the UK'. They cite a strong link between clothing longevity and repair; the findings suggest that a repair can add, on average, 1.3 years to the life of a garment.[5]

The repair techniques that I share with you in this book aren't a new solution – they're as old as the techniques used to weave the cloth in the first place, and have simply been forgotten now that convenience and throwaway culture have taken precedence over 'mend and make do' attitudes. Now more than ever, we need to shift our perspectives on repair to make sure that it is an accessible option for all, but also one that is no longer associated with any sort of class discrimination or prejudices that cause people to shy away from it.

I think it's also worth clarifying that buying new clothes isn't inherently bad. I'll always advocate for shopping second hand or vintage where possible if you need new clothing, but the reality is that people live in different locations, earn different wages and have different levels of access to shops, materials, time and education. I know it can be easy to get swept up in wanting to buy more clothing from sustainable brands so that you can get rid of any fast-fashion items, but try not to get sucked into that mindset; the most sustainable clothing options are the pieces that you already own. And when it comes to repair, I talk a lot about how every single stitch matters, and I really mean it. Whether you go on to mend one pair of jeans or half of your wardrobe when the time comes, just that subtle shift of perspective towards placing enough value on your clothing to find it worth mending will have a huge impact. It's natural, once you're aware of what happens behind closed doors in the fashion industry, to feel guilty about buying new, but I think the best mindset is to carefully consider what you're buying. If you love a piece of clothing enough to know that you'll want to cherish it and to repair it when the time comes, that's a great place to start.

How I repair

When I reached out to people for items of clothing to repair for this book, I was told countless stories of the sentimental value, the memories or the wonderful comfort and favourite fit that each of these garments brought to their owners, and it has been an honour to repair every single piece. I've used the traditional techniques that work best with every fabric and every area of damage, not only to repair, but also to celebrate the garment's journey so far.

These repair techniques are made up of small, simple stitches that are easy to learn, but hold huge power. By learning to repair your clothing you're keeping your favourite pieces in your wardrobe for longer, but you're also making a statement. By refusing to throw them away and reducing the amount you buy new, you stop contributing to the huge amounts of textiles that end up in landfill and reject the throwaway-culture mindset that has become so normal.

I know that finding the time to mend your clothes can feel like a barrier to getting started, but mending can be a valuable way to slow down and find calm among the chaos of daily life. In that sense, the mended clothing almost ends up feeling like a bonus, while the time spent focusing only on the stitches becomes a kind of meditation.

If you're a practiced sewer, then I hope that you'll find some creative inspiration from the repairs I've shown you here. And if you've ever tried to sew before and found it difficult, or if you've never used a needle and thread before, I hope visible mending will inspire you to get started, one slow stitch at a time.

1. www.theguardian.com/business/2020/nov/27/critics-slam-pretty-little-things-8p-black-friday-dress-deal
2. www.theguardian.com/fashion/2022/apr/10/shein-the-unacceptable-face-of-throwaway-fast-fashion
3. earth.org/fast-fashion-statistics/
4. clothesaid.co.uk/about-us/facts-on-clothes-recycling/
5. wrap.ngo/resources/report/citizen-insights-clothing-longevity-and-circular-business-models-receptivity-uk

How to use this book

I've put the book together with the clothing that we wear in mind. Every chapter is led by a different garment and fabric type and every technique used has been chosen based on what has worked for repairs I've done in the past.

As with any new craft or skill, practice will make a big difference to the repairs you produce, so don't be too hard on any wonky stitches – in fact, try to celebrate them! I say it repeatedly at the workshops that I teach: mended is better than perfect. Wanting to perfect a skill is no bad thing, but don't let that distract you from the bigger picture and the fact that for every item of clothing you choose to repair, it's another piece that stays out of landfill.

I've created the chart opposite so that you can see how the techniques shown in this book can be used across different fabrics and items of clothing. The main thing to think about when it comes to deciding on your repair technique is how the repair will blend into and move alongside the existing fabric. There's nothing wrong with having to add repairs over repairs, but we still want to aim for a long-lasting and durable repair in the first instance.

I use a couple of specialist terms and abbreviations in the projects shown here, which are summarized below:

RS (right side of the fabric): the outside of your clothing

WS (wrong side of the fabric): the inside of your clothing

Warp threads: the vertical threads that are the starting point for any darn

Weft threads: the horizontal threads that are woven in and out of the warp threads

Tension: how tight or loose your stitches are; getting this right helps the even structure of your stitching and the natural movement of your clothing

An important proviso for the rest of the book – I am left-handed! That means that for every technique I show you I'll always start working from left to right. If you're right-handed, you can mirror this if it's more comfortable for you to start from the right, but other than starting positions it won't affect how you work any of the techniques.

	Sashiko	Patching	Darn from front	Darn from back	Honeycomb darn	Scotch darn	Swiss darn	Seed stitch	Blanket stitch	Machine darn
Jeans / Denim										
Belt loops	x	x								x
Back pockets	x	x								x
Crotch	x	x								x
Knees	x	x	x		x	x				
Main body	x	x	x		x	x				
Jumper / Knitwear										
Underarms			x	x	x	x	x	x		
Elbows		x	x	x	x	x	x	x		
Main body		x	x	x	x	x	x	x		
Cuffs and hems		x							x	
Woven shirt										
Plackets	x	x								
Collar	x	x							x	
Underarms		x								
Edges	x	x							x	
T-shirt										
Moth holes		x	x		x	x		x	x	
Necklines	x	x							x	
Leggings										
Crotch	x		x		x			x		x
Knees	x	x	x		x			x		
Thighs	x	x	x		x			x		x
Socks										
Heels			x	x	x	x	x	x		
Soles			x	x	x	x	x	x		
Toes			x	x	x	x	x	x		
Sportswear / Outerwear										
Leather	x	x								
Technical		x								
Delicate fabrics										
Silk	x	x	x	x						

Understanding fabrics

One of the most important things to work out before you begin to mend an item of clothing is what kind of fabric you are working with. This will inform the mending method you use, and also the tools, material and considerations you will need to apply.

Woven

Woven fabrics are made on a loom and consist of vertical (warp) threads and horizontal (weft) threads. This woven structure forms the basis of several fabric types, both natural and synthetic; it is strong and durable, and can be altered at the weaving stage for a variety of finishes. There are several different weaves, such as plain weave (think cotton and linen), twill weave (think denim and drill) or satin weave (think satin and sateen fabrics).

Woven fabrics only stretch on the bias – in other words, at a diagonal to the warp and weft – as opposed to knitted fabrics, which will stretch much more easily in any direction. When using pieces of fabric for patching or reinforcement, remember to test their stretch and try to match as closely as possible to the clothing that you're repairing.

Finishing the edges of woven fabrics is also something you'll need to think about as you tackle different repairs. Folding under the edges of holes or patches gives a cleaner finish, but it will also add bulk, which may not be suitable for the repair, depending on where it is – for example, adding bulk on an underarm repair might be uncomfortable for the wearer. Leaving the edges raw can look effective, as the thread will continue to fray with wear over time, but may not be suitable for a more discreet repair.

You might find it easier to practice some techniques in the book on scrap pieces of woven fabric first, before jumping straight in with knitted fabrics. This will allow you to experiment with the techniques, different threads and stitch lengths and so on, without the added worry of how much the fabric is stretching as you work. You'll soon come to understand the natural movement of each fabric and be able to troubleshoot any tension issues as you work, but woven fabrics are definitely the easiest place to start!

Knitted

Knitted fabrics (see image opposite) are made by interlocking yarns together to create a flexible, stretchy fabric, great for T-shirts, leggings, underwear and jumpers. A benefit of knitted fabrics is that they don't fray like woven fabrics do, but they can unravel and ladder.

As with woven fabrics, there are several types of knit fabrics, from flat jersey knits (used for everything from hosiery to T-shirts and jumpers), to purl- and rib-stitch knits (used for jumpers and cardigans), right through to intarsia knits, which are multi-coloured, patterned pieces. This type of knit is used mostly for jumpers and cardigans.

Many different fibres can be used to create knitted fabrics, such as wool (lambswool, merino, alpaca), cotton, viscose, bamboo and polyester. The structure of knitted fabric also makes it great for technical clothing such as thermal base layers and sports leggings, as it can have additional properties, such as a four-way stretch.

Knitted fabrics lend themselves well to all kinds of darning techniques, depending on the clothing type and area of damage. The main thing to remember is that you don't want to completely eliminate the natural stretch of knitwear when you mend it. Many darning techniques offer flexible repairs that still allow movement within the fabric and this is really important in making sure that your repair can withstand daily wear. Using the correct needle is also especially important with knitted fabrics, as you need to make sure that as you work the needle isn't causing additional damage to the fabric by snagging the fibres or stretching the area out of shape when it is being pulled through.

Technical

A dizzying number of fabrics are available nowadays, all with different structures and finishes, and all boasting different qualities. From viscose, which is a fibre made from wood pulp, through to the array of polypropylene options (any fabric derived from oil), the chances are that your wardrobe will contain all sorts of fibres that will all need a slightly different approach when mending.

For example, pinning woven patches into place on shirts and jeans is quick and effective, but using pins on waterproof fabric or leather will create permanent holes and damage.

Similarly, when repairing sportswear or anything with extra stretch in it, you'll need to try and mimic that natural stretch as much as possible, either by matching the stretch with a patch of fabric or by using stitches that will allow an element of movement as they are worked, such as seed stitch (see pages 113–15), which is similar to an open backstitch (see page 101).

Natural vs synthetic

Woven and knitted fabrics can both be made from natural or synthetic fibres, and these will both offer different benefits. I've ended up in circular conversations about the pros and cons of natural versus synthetic many times, and there are lots of factors to take into account, from the cost of production and environmental impact of creating the fibres through to consumers' lifestyle choices.

Natural fibres, although they are naturally degradable and in theory less damaging to the planet, have been abused in their overproduction and have led to consequences such as the diminishing of the Aral Sea, mentioned earlier, due to increased demand for organic cotton, which requires a huge amount of water for its production.

Wool and leather are often off the table for those living a vegan lifestyle, although many of the alternatives for these are synthetic (plastic-based), so their inability to degrade over time is a downside. This is where I tend to come back to one of my main tips for everyone, where it's an accessible option: to shop second hand as much as possible and, more importantly, to prioritize the clothing already in your wardrobe. By prioritizing thrifting, rewearing and repairing the clothing and materials that are already in existence (and abundance!), we can make sure that those fabrics are being used to the end of their lifespan and reduce the need for further production.

UNDERSTANDING FABRICS 17

Needles

It can feel overwhelming trying to find the right sewing needles when you're getting started, as there are so many to choose from. However, it's worth knowing the various types because they all have different purposes, and good needles can make a big difference to your finished mends.

Darning needles

Darning needles come in a variety of lengths and have a long, thin eye to allow for thicker threads and yarns. Try to match the needle to the thickness of the threads you are using, and make sure it doesn't pull too much on the fabric as you pass it through. Darning needles also tend to be nice and long, which makes weaving through your warp threads when darning so much easier to do. I always turn my needle around when I'm darning so that the eye of the needle is leading the way when weaving over and under my warp threads – this is a great tip to prevent any snagging on your threads as you work. It may seem like an unnecessary extra step, but it really does make a difference when you're weaving, and I've had a lot of positive feedback about it at workshops from people who have previously struggled with darning. Ball-tipped needles are also a great option for repairing knitwear; as the name suggests, instead of a sharp point these needles have a small ball that allows you to weave in and out of the fabric without snagging or piercing the fibres.

You can also buy specific cotton darning needles and yarn darning needles, and tapestry needles are a really good option for darning with chunkier knits. They are often shorter in length but have a larger eye and a blunt tip, which is perfect for using on knitwear because they minimize the risk of fibres snagging as you stitch.

Sashiko needles

These come in a variety of lengths and often have a wider eye to allow for thicker threads, although finer-eye options are available too. They are super strong and are great for working on denim and thicker fabrics without bending or breaking. Use longer needles for straight lines of stitching (these make it much easier to create several stitches at once) and shorter needles for stitching curved lines or circles. I've never had a single sashiko needle break on me!

Other needles of note

Leather/glovers' needles have a triangular pointed tip that helps them to pierce through leather and similarly thick fabrics. Quilting needles are short and fine and useful for quick rows of whip stitch or working on more delicate fabrics. A few good general household sharps needles are always handy to have as well – I have one permanently tucked into the reel of bright orange sewing thread that I use to create basting stitches, which you'll see throughout the book.

Threads

The most important thing to remember when choosing threads to repair your clothing is to try and match the fibre content of the thread to that of the garment. For example, cotton embroidery thread will work well on cotton T-shirts, socks or even denim. Use wool threads for wool garments, and remember to take note of the care label on the garment. If you have a jumper that can be machine washed but you use a hand-wash-only mending wool for the repair, it is likely to shrink or felt in the wash, which will pucker the garment. If you're struggling to find a perfect match, at the very least aim to match natural fibres to natural fabrics and synthetic fibres to synthetic fabrics.

Darning threads

From crochet cotton to darning wools and embroidery threads, there are many options that can be used for darning. Embroidery threads are a great starting point, as they are generally 100 percent cotton (always double check this) and come in a huge variety of colours. Their six strands can be split into different weights to match the clothing you're repairing, which will mean a more comfortable darned patch. They also wash well and won't shrink, though they can have a slight sheen to them, whereas mending wools and yarns don't.

Sashiko threads

There's a variety of threads to choose from for sashiko, from sashiko-specific cotton threads to crochet cotton and embroidery threads. Sashiko thread and crochet cotton are preferable because they are twisted, not stranded, so they don't split like embroidery threads do and will be more hardwearing on fabrics like denim. They have a matte finish.

Different weights of sashiko threads are available, from fine to medium, to allow for the best finish on the clothing you are stitching. Sashiko cotton is really nice to work with and gives a great finish, especially on denim. Crochet cotton or perle cotton, which is twisted, also works really well and might give you a wider variety of colour options; I also like to use it for darning if the weight matches with fabric I'm repairing.

Other threads

Although I don't use them often, silk mending threads are also a popular option, and come in lots of beautiful shades and weights. (I don't use silk unless it's second hand because I'm vegetarian; creating silk yarn kills the silkworm in the process.) If you have access to local second-hand shops, charity shops, flea markets or other online markets like eBay, then you can often find bundles of threads (often knitting leftovers or embroidery project cast-offs) fairly cheaply. It's always worth scouting these out to build up a collection of threads that you can source from to suit any mending project. This is another benefit of visible mending: your only limitation is the fibre content and weight of the thread, and you can have fun choosing a new colour palette for the repair and item of clothing.

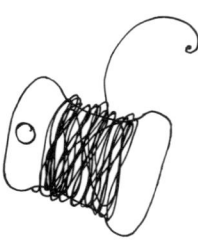

Other supplies

Thimbles

These are a really useful addition to your mending tool library, especially for sashiko, as working through several layers of fabric or thick denim can be tough on your hands. Having worked on lots of pairs of jeans over the years, I recommend a fingertip thimble (1) and a palm thimble – your fingers will thank you for it! There are many different types available, from traditional metal fingertip thimbles to silicone grips and leather palm thimbles.

Scissors

Small, sharp embroidery scissors (2) are great when working on small mends, but any scissors will do, as long as they are sharp enough to cut threads easily without fraying them. Pinking shears (3) are also handy when working with fabric scraps for patching. They aren't essential, but I always use them to trim my fabric patches to size, as they help minimize fraying and leave a nice clean finish on the inside of mends.

Iron

An iron will come in handy more often than you might think when repairing your clothes, so make sure to keep one close at hand. From prepping patches and fabrics before mending to the final press on a finished repair, a hot iron can really help you achieve a high-quality mend, so don't skip that step!

Fabric pens

Chalk pencils or fabric markers are another useful tool for mending, and can be really helpful for marking out the pattern of your repair before you start. Chalk will rub or wash off clothing easily, but alternatively you can use fabric markers with ink that will either iron off (such as Pilot Frixion pens) or can be removed with water in the wash. If using a fabric marker, it's always best to test them on an unseen area of clothing first to make sure that they don't stain or fade the fabric.

To use alongside chalk or pens, there are tons of templates out there that can be used for transferring sashiko patterns onto your fabric. I designed my own range in three different styles that I use frequently when working with sashiko, and I love that they enable you to get sewing more quickly!

Darning mushrooms

Darning mushrooms and discs (4) were traditionally used for darning holes in socks, but they can be used with other items of clothing too, and will help you keep the right tension as you darn. If you don't have one, look around your house: you can always use a ramekin, a doorknob or a jam jar lid instead. Using an elastic tie or a hairband around your mushroom or darning tool will also help keep the tension of your fabric while you're darning – plus it means you can put the work down and stop halfway through if need be, without worrying about your threads going slack. Make sure not to pull fabrics too tightly across your darning mushroom when tying into place, as this will pull the fabric and the darn out of shape.

It's helpful to have a few different shapes to hand: darning mushrooms tend to have a domed top, which makes them great for darning socks or other shaped areas of fabric where you want to mimic the body's natural curves. Darning discs tend to be flatter, which means that they will work well for any flat areas of clothing such as elbows and sleeves, and they have a groove on the side to make it easier to secure a hairband or elastic band into place.

Darning looms

Several old-fashioned darning looms became popular in the early-to-mid-20th century, and the Speedweve (5) has become most well known over the last few years. Other versions, such as the Sellar's Rapid Darner and the Ebor Darner, are also noteworthy, and during my treasure hunting over several years I've managed to acquire a few different types. Despite their interesting history and their benefits when using, I don't consider them to be an essential tool for darning, and I don't want people to think that they can't get started without one. Darning is a wonderfully simple technique that doesn't need these extra gadgets when you're just starting out! That said, there are beautiful replicas being made today all over the world by some awesome small businesses, so if you do decide that you'd like to add one to your collection and can't find one second hand, then these are a great option.

Other tools

There are a few other items that I'd recommend – none are essential, but they can be helpful.

A latch hook or crochet hook (6) to repair ladders in knitted fabrics. A latch hook is a clever tool that has a small arm that makes it easier to pick up and catch stitches, but a crochet hook will work just as well. They come in several different sizes/thicknesses to match different weights of fabrics.

A magnifying lamp and light to help with delicate techniques such as Swiss darning, or when working with fine fabrics like silk.

Hairbands or elastic bands to hold fabric in place as you darn. I recommend having a stash of hairbands to hand because the fabric coating on them eliminates the snagging that can happen with elastic bands.

Sewing clips or paper clips (7) to use instead of pins or basting stitches when working on technical or leather fabrics.

A tailor's ham.

Only one of the repairs shown in this book requires a sewing machine and this is the machine darning technique shown on jean crotches in Chapter 1. While the other hand-sewn techniques shown for denim can be applied here, machine darning is the strongest option for a comfortable and durable repair and so the option I would recommend. See page 60 for more details.

Introduction to darning

Darning is a method of repairing holes in fabric by weaving interlocking threads with a needle to create, in effect, a new patch of fabric over the holes. Throughout history, darning has been an essential but often undervalued technique. Mostly invisible, it would have been crucial in hiding a patch and area of damage so as not to draw attention to someone's lack of wealth. Darning from the back (see page 74) was a commonly used technique to help blend the repair into the rest of the clothing. As clothing and fabrics were much more valuable and wardrobes consisted of far fewer items than today's do, repairing what you had was the first port of call, and choosing to buy new was a privilege. Darning was such a commonplace skill that it was taught in schools, where children were expected to create samplers of several different darning techniques.

Darning is a brilliant, multi-purpose mending skill, with many techniques to choose from, which can be worked across a variety of fabrics and clothing types. A standard, woven darned patch mimics the appearance and structure of woven fabrics, but (as with other methods of darning) it can be used across various types of fabrics. You can also make colourful patches with darning by using different-coloured warp and weft threads, even alternating how many rows you work in each colour to create checked patterns.

All the darning techniques have their own specific qualities, and some work better on certain fabrics or areas of damage than others. They include:

Plain weave (also known as basket weave or sometimes Oxford weave)

A standard plain-weave darn uses the same process as the larger weaving looms that are used to create fabric, just on a much smaller scale! A standard plain-weave darn is made up of vertical warp threads (1) that have horizontal weft threads woven through them (2), and looks great on woven fabrics and knit fabrics alike.

Once you're comfortable with the basic structure of a plain weave, you can start to create different weave patterns. For example, a twill weave is created by weaving over two warps, then under two warps, across a row, and then for every subsequent row shifting that pattern across by one (3). A herringbone weave uses the structure of a twill weave, but then doubles back on itself after several rows to create a zig-zag effect (4).

Swiss darning (or duplicate stitch)

This is a knitwear-specific technique that recreates the looped structure of a knitted garment by making new loops that interlock with the surrounding knit stitches, and if done with matching threads can end up blending in seamlessly with the rest of the fabric. Swiss darning is a great technique to use over thinned-out areas of knitted fabric before a hole appears, but can also be worked to cover a hole, using either pins (5) or a series of grafting stitches (6, 7) to hold and build up new stitches. (When looking at your fabric, try to pick out the rows of Vs on the outside of the mend – these are the stitches that you'll be replicating for the duplicate stitch.)

The technique works really well (and is simplest) on thicker knitwear, but can be very

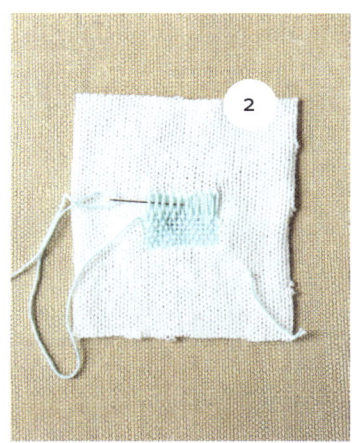

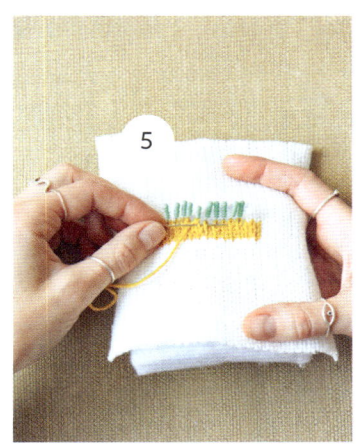

INTRODUCTION TO DARNING 25

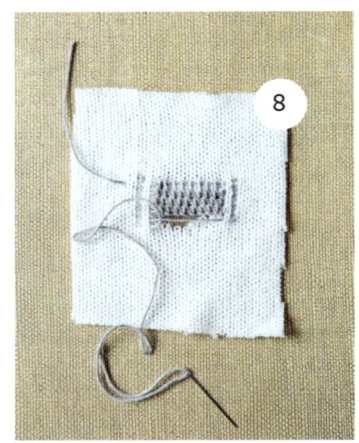

A really strong method of darning that's great for high-stress areas.

INTRODUCTION 26

time consuming and tricky to achieve on fine knits or socks, where the individual stitches are harder to see. I'd also recommend starting out on lighter-coloured fabrics when you first start to work the technique, as they'll be much easier to see and follow.

QUICK TIP: Rather than a darning disc or mushroom it's best to use a soft pincushion, a tailor's ham or even a sponge if you're using pins when Swiss darning. If you decide to use grafting stitches, then a harder darning mushroom will work fine. I recommend experimenting with both options if you can; I struggled with Swiss darning for a while when using grafting stitches, and the technique became much easier for me when using pins, but I know others who have found the opposite. As with all the techniques shown in the book, find your own comfort within each one and adapt as necessary. And never underestimate how much difference practice can make! With every darn and repair I do I learn something new about the best ways to achieve a strong result, so don't be put off if your first attempts are wonky.

Scotch darning

This uses blanket stitches worked in rows to create a strong square patch that looks more like crochet than darning (8, 9). It's a really strong method of darning that's great for high-stress areas such as elbows.

Honeycomb darning

Honeycomb darning is a variation of a blanket stitch worked in the round to create a really flat darn that works from both the front and back of the fabric. This darn is a very good option for reinforcing threadbare fabrics before a hole has worn through, for example on the heel of a sock or even leggings; the technique will look different when repairing thinned-out fabrics in this way (10) as opposed to filling a hole (11 and its reverse, 11R), in which case the stitches will be much denser.

In both Scotch and honeycomb darning, stitches are made by inserting your needle and thread through each loop of thread as you make it; catching the loop interlocks the threads together. This can seem counter-intuitive at first! When working these techniques you can either position your thread underneath your needle as you make each stitch, thereby ensuring you create a loop of thread to catch every time, or as you pull your thread through for each stitch you can stop when there is a small loop left showing and then insert your needle and thread through to catch the loop. Both options work well, although I tend to favour the first as I find it allows for a smoother sewing practice.

ONE FINAL TIP: It's important at the end of each row of darning to leave enough slack in the thread to allow for movement in the darn when the clothing is stretched. Pulling too tightly between each row will cause stress to the fabric and create a puckered darn that does not lie flat against the clothing.

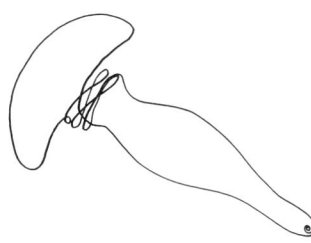

Introduction to sashiko

Sashiko (meaning 'little stabs') is a traditional Japanese embroidery technique that can be used to decorate, reinforce and mend fabrics. The technique was used during the Edo period (1603–1867) and traditionally used white cotton thread and indigo-dyed cotton cloth to work over in patches to reinforce holes or worn-through fabrics.

Sashiko was standard practice for clothing and textiles to ensure their long lifespan; layer upon layer of fabrics and stitches (known as boro) were used to reinforce, patch and revive textiles to ensure that they would survive generations of family members.

As with darning, sashiko was a practice that was born out of necessity. The need to keep clothing in circulation for as long as possible meant that every scrap of fabric was highly valuable and worth using, and the dense patterns of stitching strongly reinforced it.

Sashiko has seen a resurgence in recent years, especially as a form of visible mending, and it's easy to see why when you look back to historical examples. It is beautiful in its simplicity: a basic running stitch with the freedom to create dozens of patterns and styles makes it a really accessible mending technique for beginners.

Another factor that makes sashiko accessible is that it can be adapted for most woven fabrics, and works particularly well on denim. The combination of sashiko thread with denim creates a really bold finish, and it's a great way to mend high-stress areas of denim such as the knee area of jeans. While the traditional white cotton thread and indigo cloth is still very impactful (and mostly how I prefer to work) there are now all sorts of

coloured and variegated threads that you can use to create bold and modern repairs.

Sashiko can be worked either freehand or by using stencils and chalk, fabric markers or pre-printed fabric to stitch over. I personally love both methods: following the shape of a hole with organic patches of freehand stitching looks so striking, but there is equally something special about the effect of a sashiko pattern such as the *Shippou Tsunagi* (Seven Treasures) worked across a denim jacket. Following pre-drawn or printed lines when starting out can make the process a lot easier.

There are many other traditional repair techniques specific to different cultures, all with their own stories and heritages. Kantha, for example, is an Indian technique that uses similar techniques of layering and patching scraps of fabrics to repair and reinforce. As always, I'd recommend learning as much as you can about the history of these techniques in more detail to really appreciate their origins.

Using both hands and the fabric itself will help you find a rhythm.

INTRODUCTION 30

Practical sashiko tips

Sashiko relies on creating lines of very even stitches. The general rule is to aim for stitches about the length of a grain of rice – or around 2 stitches per centimetre (6 stitches per inch) – and the gaps between them should be around half the stitch length. You will find your own comfortable stitch length with practice, and you can also make adjustments depending on whether you're stitching freehand or following a sashiko template. The long needles used for sashiko allow you to do several stitches at once, which helps make them even.

Using both hands and the needle and fabric itself will help you find a rhythm. In sashiko this movement is called *Unshin*. You can use your hand holding the needle and thread as an anchor, and your other hand to direct and push the fabric onto the needle as you make several stitches. Practicing a few rows of straight stitches lets you experiment and find a comfortable stitch length for you, and the more you practice, the more stitches you'll be able to pick up on your needle in one go. As with darning, it's important not to pull the threads too taut as you are stitching, or between rows. Aim for a little slack between each row to create a repair that sits naturally with the rest of the fabric and allows freedom of movement for the wearer.

When sewing, try to keep your needle and thread on top of the fabric as you work, so you don't have to turn the garment inside out as you sew. This is especially helpful for hard-to-access areas like knees, as it can be fiddly to keep turning the jeans leg in and out.

Use longer sashiko needles for stitching straight lines and patterns (1), as they allow you to pick up several stitches on the needle at once, and shorter ones for stitching curves and circles (2) so that you can create smooth curved lines. When stitching circular designs, I find it's best to pick up 1–2 stitches at a time to ensure a smooth curved finish.

The more you practice, the more stitches you'll be able to pick up.

Introduction to patching

Patching is a great catch-all technique for most types of clothing repair, and there are several ways to get creative and make it your own. The main thing to remember is to use fabric pieces that are of a similar weight and fibre content to the clothing. For example, if you're covering a hole in a pair of jeans, you'll need to use a similar weight denim or heavyweight cotton fabric piece to ensure that the repair withstands future wear; a stretchy or knitted fabric piece wouldn't work, or at least it wouldn't last very long and could cause further strain to the existing fabric.

Practical patching tips

You can choose to place a fabric patch on the inside or outside of your clothing, and you can leave the edges raw or folded under. If you fold under the edges of a patch (1), for example on the outside of your clothing, remember to take into account the bulk that will be added by doing this. It will work better on some fabrics than others, and it's also important to think about where the damage is and how that patch will affect the wearer – for example, a thick patch applied to the elbow of a shirt may restrict movement and flexibility. If you don't fold under the edges, cutting the patch with pinking shears can help prevent fraying.

Throughout the book I will refer to 'basting' patches into place as an alternative option to pinning them. Basting stitches are long stitches that hold the patch in place securely, often worked in a bright coloured thread (2); they are then removed when your repair stitches are complete. You can use pins instead (3), but depending on the size and placement of the damage on your clothing, basting can be preferable, as there's less chance of being pricked while you're sewing!

Blanket stitch

Blanket stitch (1) crops up a few times in this book because it can be used in so many ways for repairs, and is a really effective way to secure a fabric patch into place. Scotch darning (see page 27) uses blanket stitch worked in stacked straight rows to cover a hole, and produces a strong form of darning that is great for high-stress areas such as elbows. Honeycomb darning uses the same technique, but is worked in circles.

Other than the blanket stitch, a simple whip stitch (see page 44) is my main go-to for patches, as I like the finish it gives on both sides of the fabric. This stitch is worked by sewing through both layers of fabric and over the edge of the fabric patch (4) to secure it into place.

Starting & finishing your repair

Before you get started on a repair, allow yourself a little creative thinking space. Decide on what kind of repair you'd like to create based on the garment and where the damage is. Is this a subtle area to mend or somewhere to make a statement? Think about the fabric content and whether the area needs a lot of movement, such as a knee or elbow. Sometimes it's helpful to sketch out a few design ideas to see what feels best and help you visualize the scale of your repair. Drawing ideas out can also take the pressure off those first few stitches, as it means you already know how you want the finished repair to look.

Whichever mending technique you use, whether on woven or knitted fabrics or on socks or shirts, you should always aim to make your repair at least 1 centimetre (⅜ inch) bigger (if not more), all around, than the damage itself. If you begin stitching into weakened and damaged fabric you will run into problems and the repair won't be strong enough to withstand wear and tear. It may take a little more time to do, but creating a larger patch will ensure a secure and long-lasting repair.

Before you make those first stitches, make sure you have all the tools needed to work on the repair at hand, and prepare your clothing by removing any loose or frayed threads before you start. Cut your thread at a comfortable length and thread your needle. A comfortable thread length to cut and work with tends to be about the length of your arm from wrist to shoulder. This is long enough to make sure that you aren't having to join in several new lengths of thread on a repair (and therefore have more ends to weave in at the end), but not so long that the thread is likely to knot and tangle as you are working. There are countless tips for

needle threading out there but I tend to fold the thread in half over the needle, then pull this off and push the folded loop through the eye of the needle - this technique means less chance of frayed ends.

If using, insert a darning disc, mushroom or tailor's ham on the inside of your garment and secure it into position with a hairband or an elastic band, remembering not to stretch out or distort your clothing. If you aren't using anything underneath your fabric, you'll need to make sure that as you work you are only sewing through the top layer of your fabric and not through to the back of your jumper or jeans! You might find it most comfortable to sew with one hand inside the garment, or alternatively you could always insert a piece of cardboard or a book in between the layers.

When starting and finishing a repair you have the choice to knot off the ends of your threads or to weave them into the repair.

For comfort and longevity, and especially on knitted fabrics, weaving in the ends is the preferable option and is a secure and discreet way to finish a repair. However, knotting definitely still has its place and, for baggy clothing or fabrics that won't be worn close to the skin, knotting the ends off is fine, and works well for denim. The main thing to remember with knots is that they limit the movement of the repair. If you choose to use them, you'll want to leave enough slack on the tail threads to allow flexibility because, if pulled too tightly, the tail threads and knot can distort the repair and subsequently the clothing as it is worn.

For most repairs, I tend to insert my needle a little way away from the side of the damage and then leave a tail thread (about the length of my hand) to weave in at the end. However, you can also weave in the tail threads as you start your repair for a flat and knot-free finish. To do this, sew a few stitches in the opposite direction to where you intend to start and pull your thread all the way through, leaving just the end showing on the top of your fabric. Then, switching direction to start work, stitch back across these stitches, catching them as you go. You can then pull the thread through and continue stitching, and your tail thread will be embedded securely in your stitching.

When it comes to finishing repairs by weaving in the ends, I use the same weaving-in options regardless of the fabric I'm using, and whether I have used darning or sashiko techniques. On the wrong side of the fabric, you can either weave the tail threads in and out, picking up just a few stitches in one direction and then working back the other way two or three times. This creates a small squiggle of thread that lies flat against the fabric and can't be seen on the outside of the clothing (as on page 30, image bottom right). The other option is to weave the tail threads in and out of a few of the stitches from your repair, but if choosing this option make sure that you don't pull or snag the stitches in any way, as this can alter the tension on the finished repair on the right side of your clothing.

Decide on what kind of repair you'd like to create based on the garment and where the damage is.

Troubleshooting: problems to look out for

As you start to mend different items of clothing and use different repair techniques, you'll begin to find comfortable pairings of fabric type to technique. However, even when you have a perfect match of fabric, thread and technique, you might still come across problems. Here are a few of the most common problems I've found, and why they happen. Don't be afraid to unpick a repair and start again if it isn't working out; it's better to undo the repair at this stage rather than pushing through and creating a repair that will cause more damage to the clothing, or not last very well.

DARNING

Gaps in the finished darn

This can happen when the warp threads or weft threads (or sometimes both) are too far apart. Aim for the distance between the threads to be about the same width as the thread you are using for an evenly filled darned patch. It could also be that the yarn you've chosen to use is too fine for the clothing – remember to try and match the weight.

Puckered darn

This is likely caused by the clothing being pulled too tightly over the darning mushroom or disc. This stretches out the fabric, meaning that once you remove the darning mushroom, the darn you created will pucker up and not lie flat to the fabric underneath.

Floating darn

A floating darn is one that has been woven without securing each weft row at the sides. Securing every weft row at the edge of the warp threads ensures that the darned patch is attached to the fabric all the way around and helps it to blend into the original fabric. These securing stitches also encase the hole on the reverse side of the clothing, meaning that even if the hole continues to unravel, it will not be able to extend past these stitches.

PATCHING

Clothing feels bulky once patched
This could be caused by using a fabric patch that is too heavy for the clothing. Always try to match the fabric weight to the clothing and, if patching in an area close to other seams, avoid folding the patch edges under, which will create extra bulk.

Clothing feels stretched around the patch/patch is baggy at the centre
The fabric patch may have moved around during sewing, which can lead to either the clothing being pulled out of shape or the patch being loose at the centre. When pinning or basting the fabric patch into place, remember to check that the patch and clothing lie flat to each other and continue to check this as you work on the repair.

SASHIKO

Inconsistent stitch length
Creating even stitches with sashiko takes practice, but using a fabric marker to draw out the stitching lines first can help. You might also find that picking up fewer stitches at a time helps you focus on creating the same stitch length each time.

Puckered stitching
This happens when the thread is pulled too tightly between each row. Remember to leave a little slack or loop of thread between each row of stitching. After every few rows, give your clothing a quick stretch in all directions to make sure that the stitches have room to move.

Caring for your repairs

As your wardrobe starts to fill up with a unique tapestry of repairs, you'll want to make sure that the repairs last for as long as possible. For the most part, when the techniques are all applied correctly according to the clothing and fabric type, you can continue washing and wearing your clothes as normal.

With wool items, though, it's important to factor in how you'll wash them once repaired. For example, if you have a wool mix jumper that previously has been fine in the washing machine, but you have repaired it using a 100 percent mending wool, you'll need to handwash the jumper from now on. Trust me when I say that it's super disappointing to find out that a beautiful darn you've spent time working on has felted in the wash!

For denim, the repairs should be fairly low-maintenance and not require any different washing methods, but it's worth checking how your woven-in tail threads and patches are holding up over time. If you've used pinking shears on your patches then you shouldn't have to worry about this at all, but if the edges are left totally raw you may need to snip a few frayed ends every now and then. I've also never had any issues with any tail threads unravelling – even on high-stress areas such as the knees – but again, keep an eye out as they continue to be worn and washed.

As mentioned previously, creating repairs that are at least 1 centimetre (⅜ inch) bigger than the damage on clothing is the best way to reinforce the fabric and create a long-lasting repair. But with time and continued wear, you may notice new holes appearing next to or in a similar place to the originals, especially for those high-wear areas (knees, elbows, crotch and so on) If the time comes when you need to repair an existing repair, try to view the original repair as part of the original fabric and don't let it interfere with your new repair where possible. Layered-up repairs are some of my favourites to look at, as you can see the story of wear that has built up on the clothing.

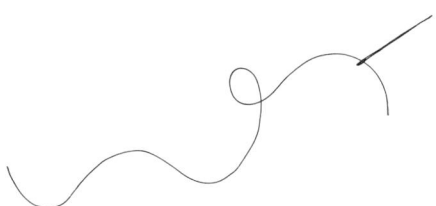

When not to mend: a note before we begin

As much as I want this book to inspire you to tackle all sorts of clothing damage, there will of course be times when a piece of clothing is beyond repair. It's a personal call to make, but here are a few things that I keep in mind when approaching a new project.

Is the damage from wear and tear or accidental?

For example, if you accidentally snag a T-shirt and make a hole, but the rest of the top is in good condition, then it's absolutely worth repairing and the hole itself should be fairly straightforward to fix, as you won't have to tackle thinned or worn-out areas of fabric as well as the hole.

How old is the clothing?

If the clothing is so old that it has worn thin but you still love to wear it, then I think it's worth repairing, even if it becomes a bit of a project. If moths have been at your favourite jumper but you can repair the damage (and work to treat the moth problem in your wardrobe!) then yes, repair it. And if the same pair of jeans that you live in keeps wearing out at the knees or back pockets, but you can patch, stitch and add layers to keep them in action – you guessed it, repair it!

What is the clothing made from?

If the fabric quality isn't great, which means that the garment has become too fragile to wear, the repairs aren't holding up or you aren't wearing it any more because it feels uncomfortable or doesn't fit, then I'd say don't repair it. If you can donate it to someone who can use it, or if you can cut the fabric up into scraps for cleaning or other uses, sometimes that's the best option. Building up a box of fabric scraps is great if you can do it – this book covers several types of patching techniques, all of which have been done using odds and ends of beyond-repair clothing. It's unavoidable that clothes will eventually reach the end of their life cycle, and it can be harder to part with clothes that you've spent time repairing, but don't waste your time and energy repairing things that you no longer wear and love, or that are so far gone that they spend more time in your mending pile than out of it.

Patch, stitch and add layers to keep clothes in action.

How often is it worn?

Again, if the clothing in question is a staple that you find yourself wearing daily, weekly or monthly, then taking the time to repair it definitely seems worth it. However, if you've found it languishing away in the back of your wardrobe – maybe it doesn't fit as well any more, or maybe the style doesn't suit you – then I think it's important to factor in your time. The time it takes to repair something can either be a joy or an annoyance, and I've found that the annoyance tends to occur when you're spending time working on something that you don't fully enjoy afterwards. Carving out pockets of time to focus on clothing repair is often one of the biggest hurdles, so make sure that the clothing is worth it for you.

Has it been repaired before, and how many times? Is it breaking in the same areas?

I've been asked a few times if I think it's worth repairing fast-fashion pieces or clothes that were cheap to begin with. Often the fabric quality isn't great, and if garment workers are being forced into dangerous working conditions, it should come as no shock that this could also impact the quality of the construction. The programme 'Inside the Shein Machine: Untold', shown on Channel 4 in the UK in 2022, uncovered that in some fast fashion retailers' Chinese factories, workers could get paid as little as 0.27 yuan (3 UK pence or 4 US cents) per garment produced, and are expected to make up to 500 items a month.[1] This is not an environment conducive to making clothing that's intended to last. I'm not placing blame here in any way on the workers themselves, but on a totally unsustainable industry.

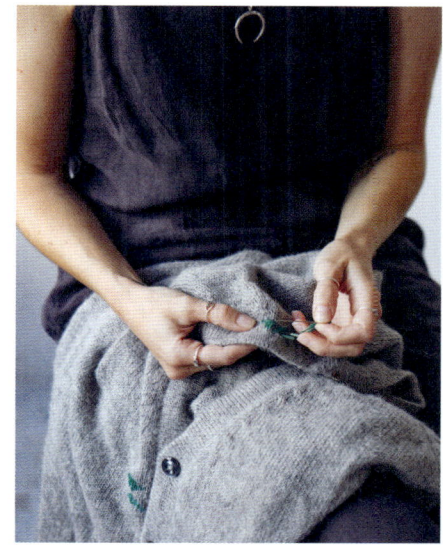

Despite all of these factors, the same questions still apply for me: it's not about how cheap something was to start with, it's about how the clothing makes you feel and how much time you need to put into repairing it. If it's a favourite staple piece in your wardrobe or something that makes you super happy to wear it, that to me marks its real value.

1. www.channel4.com/programmes/inside-the-shein-machine-untold

1 *Jeans*

Denim is such a versatile fabric and is undoubtedly a staple in modern wardrobes. Traditionally used for workwear, it's a strong and hard-wearing fabric that is great at being put through its paces no matter what you're wearing it for.

Woven in construction using a twill weave, there are many options when it comes to repairing denim. From sashiko to patching and even darning, its durability means that it can withstand a variety of mending techniques and provides a great base for experimenting with really creative repairs.

Main body

A contrasting piece of denim applied underneath and stitched into place following the shape of the hole is a strong and really eye-catching repair. Folding the edges of the hole under gives a clean finish, and the stitching works to reinforce the edges of the hole while also securing the fabric patch underneath. These whip stitches look similar to blanket stitch, and are great for adding strength in a quick, simple way.

This kind of patch can be used on any area of your jeans, but I think it works really well on the holes that develop where front pockets are, often caused by a phone or keys wearing down the denim from the inside over time.

If your jeans have any stretch to them, the fabric patch will also need an element of stretch, especially if used in a high stress area such as the knees. If you don't have a suitable piece of fabric for this, you can place a regular denim piece under the hole but positioned on the bias (in other words, diagonally at a 45-degree angle), allowing the fabric patch more movement.

My mend:
Wear and tear to the front pocket area, fixed with a patch and whip stitch

You will need:
A fabric patch big enough to allow at least a 1-cm (3/8-in) margin all round the hole
A sashiko needle
Sashiko cotton thread
Basting thread and a hand sewing needle or pins

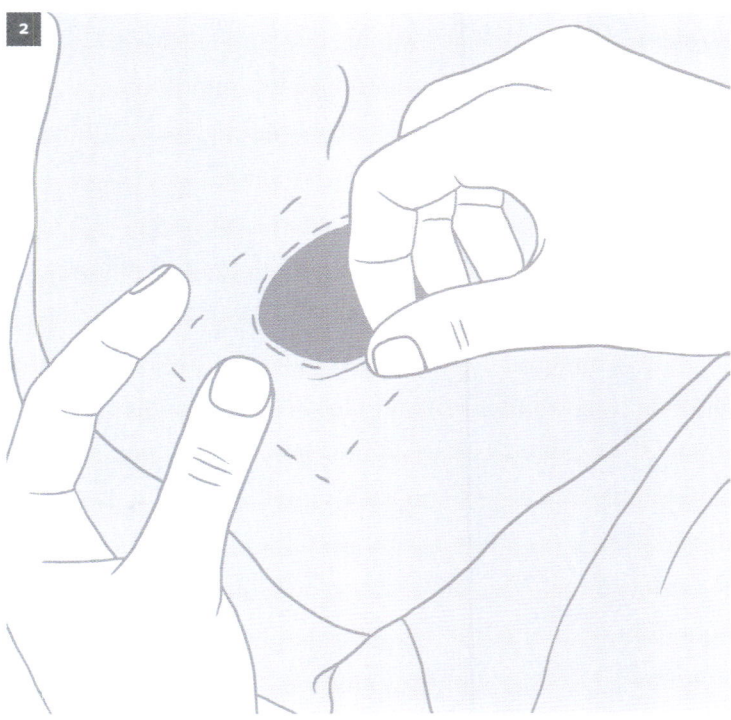

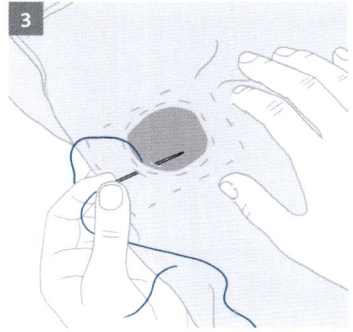

1. Trim any loose or frayed edges around the hole. Turn the jeans inside out (WS), then either baste or pin your fabric patch into place on the inside (WS) of your jeans, placing it with the right side facing down. Take your time here and make sure that both the jeans and the patch are lying nice and flat, and that the grain of the patch fabric is lying in the same direction as that of the jeans (you can use the direction of the twill/diagonal weave to check this).

2. Turn your jeans right side out (RS). At this point, you can also choose to fold under the edges of the hole and baste them into place as shown above, or you can fold the edges under bit by bit as you stitch your way around the hole. If the hole is fairly circular or small, you might find it helpful to snip just a few millimetres into the edges evenly around the hole to make it easier to fold the edges under.

3. Thread your needle and insert it at the seam edge of the jeans near the patch (RS), then bring it up into position through the fabric patch next to the folded edge of the hole. Leave a tail of thread on the outside (RS) of the jeans to be woven in at the end.

MAIN BODY 45

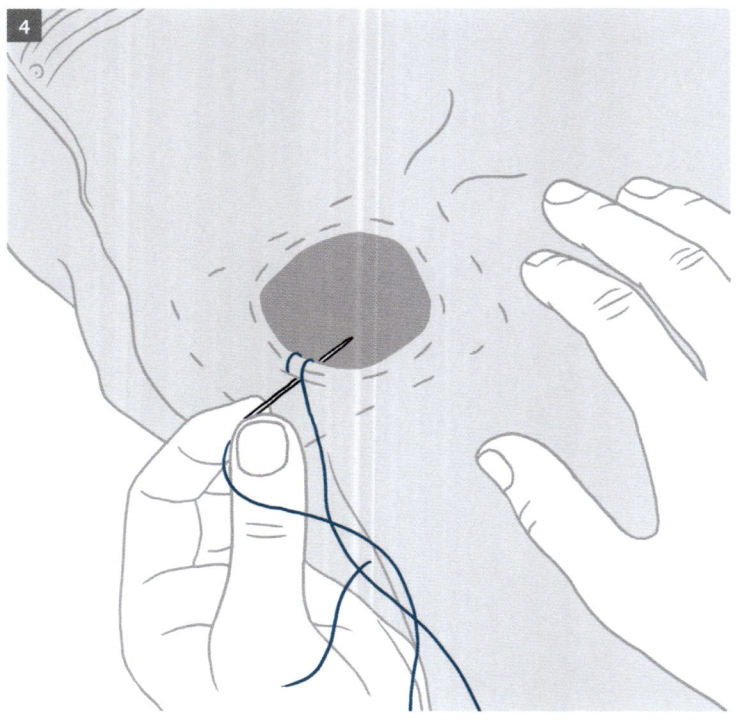

4. Push your needle down through the jeans fabric to make your first stitch, then up again along from the first stitch, bringing your needle back up into position through the patch close to the folded edge of the hole. You want these stitches to be around 5mm–1cm (¼–⅜in) in length and evenly spaced.

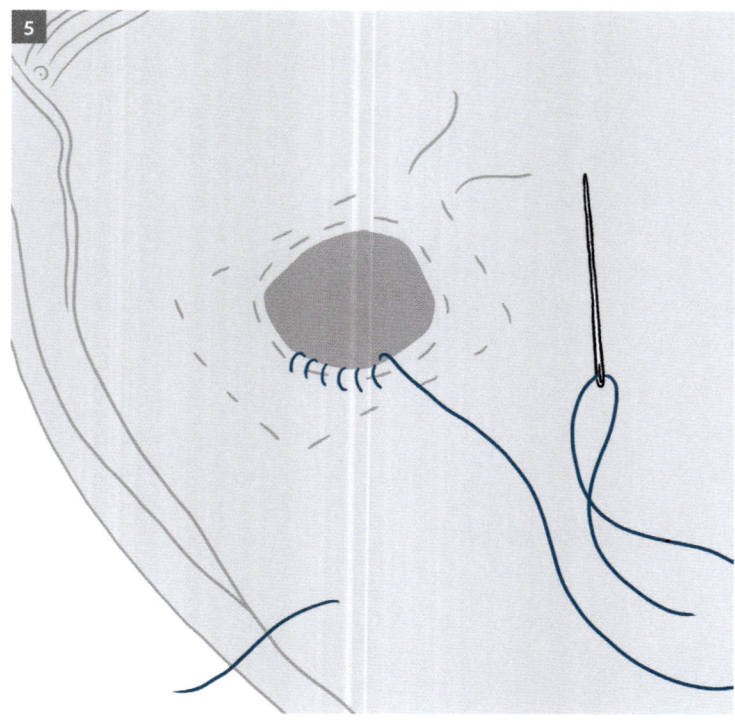

5. Repeat step 4, working around the shape of the hole and creating similarly sized and spaced stitches to secure the folded edge of the jeans to the patch fabric underneath. Keep working around the hole, ensuring that you are stitching the jeans to the patch fabric.

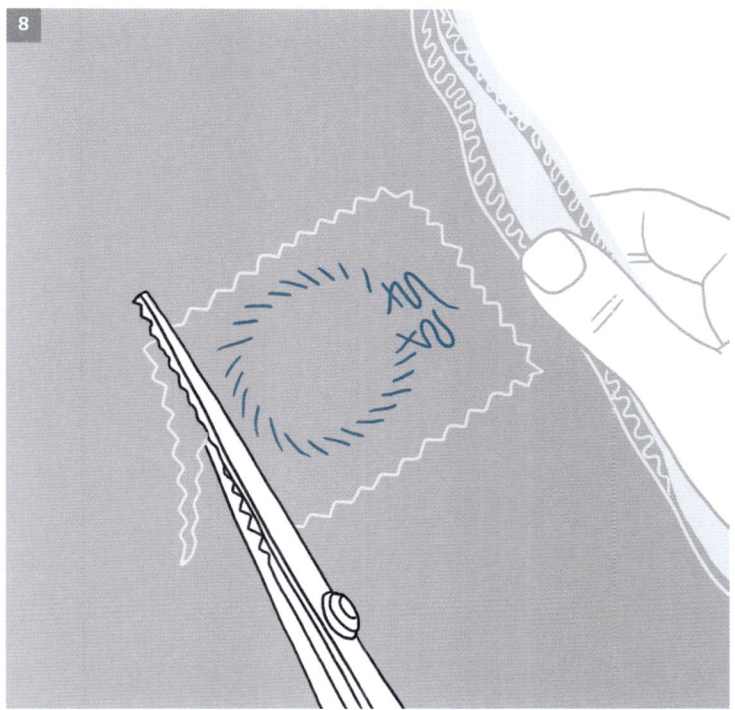

6. If you run out of thread while you are working, simply pull your needle through to the inside (WS) of the jeans after finishing a stitch and leave the tail thread to secure later on. You can then start working with a new length of thread in the same way as you did at the beginning of step 3.

7. When you come back round to the first stitch, allow enough room to create a last stitch that is evenly spaced between the others. Make this final stitch, then push your needle down and out to the side of the jeans, as you did at the beginning.

8. Carefully snip the basting stitches to remove them. Pull the tail threads through to the inside (WS) of the jeans and weave them in to secure them (see page 35). If your patch is too big you can now also trim it down, preferably with pinking shears – just don't cut too close to the stitches. Try to leave a margin of about 1cm (⅜ in) all around.

Knees

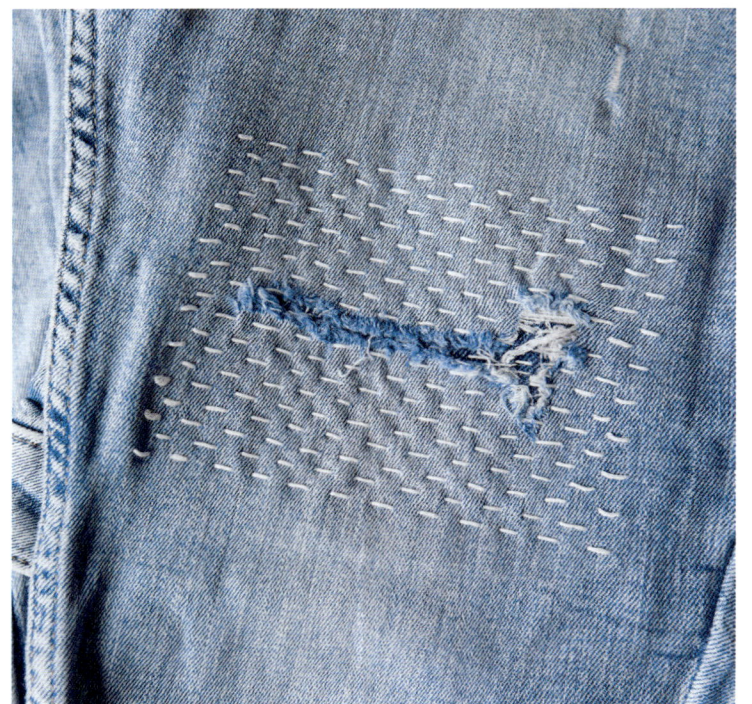

You will need:
A fabric patch big enough to allow at least a 1-cm (³⁄₈-in) margin all round the hole
A sashiko needle
Sashiko cotton thread
Basting thread and a hand-sewing needle or pins
A thimble
A fabric marker or chalk pencil
A ruler or stitching template

You can use a similar technique to that on pages 44–7 for the knees of jeans by using a patch underneath in the same way, but keeping the frayed edges raw. In this example, I have used a series of running stitches all around the hole on the knee to secure the patch into place and worked over the frayed edges instead of folding them under, to avoid too much bulk. I love the effect of this kind of repair – the combination of frayed denim and sashiko thread works beautifully, as everything is held in place but the denim continues to wear at the edges with use and washing. Most importantly, the series of running stitches around the hole not only holds the patch in place underneath, but also adds further strength and reinforcement, while allowing freedom of movement when the jeans are worn.

My mend:
A worn-through knee patched with denim underneath and sashiko

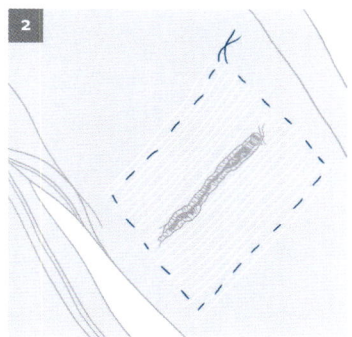 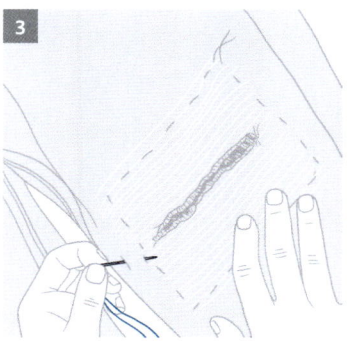 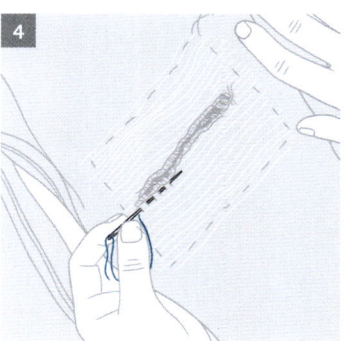

1. Turn the jeans inside out (WS). Cut a fabric patch to size and baste it into position on the inside (WS) of your jeans, remembering to position it with the right side facing down.

2. Turn the jeans right side out and mark out a grid or series of lines using a fabric marker or chalk and a ruler or template. I usually aim for lines spaced 1cm (⅜in) apart, but you can choose the spacing you like.

3. Using your marker lines to guide you, push your needle down and through at the side of the patch and then up into position on a line to make your first stitch. Leave a tail of thread on the RS of the jeans to be woven in at the end.

NOTE: To make sure that the fabric patch stays in place and avoid a lumpy finish, I find it easiest to start your stitches in the middle of your marked lines, right next to the rip on the jeans, and work down in one direction to fill in the remaining lines. Then go back with a new length of thread and fill in the top rows. This works well for any large mend or mends on stretchy material.

4. Push the needle down through the fabric to make your first stitch, only pushing it through a short way, then bring it straight back up again to start your next stitch. You're aiming for even stitches, each the size of a grain of rice. Carry on stitching along your line collecting as many stitches on your needle at once as feels comfortable. If you have a long needle, you can make between 3 and 5 stitches at once. A thimble can be super helpful here to help push your needle through the layers of denim.

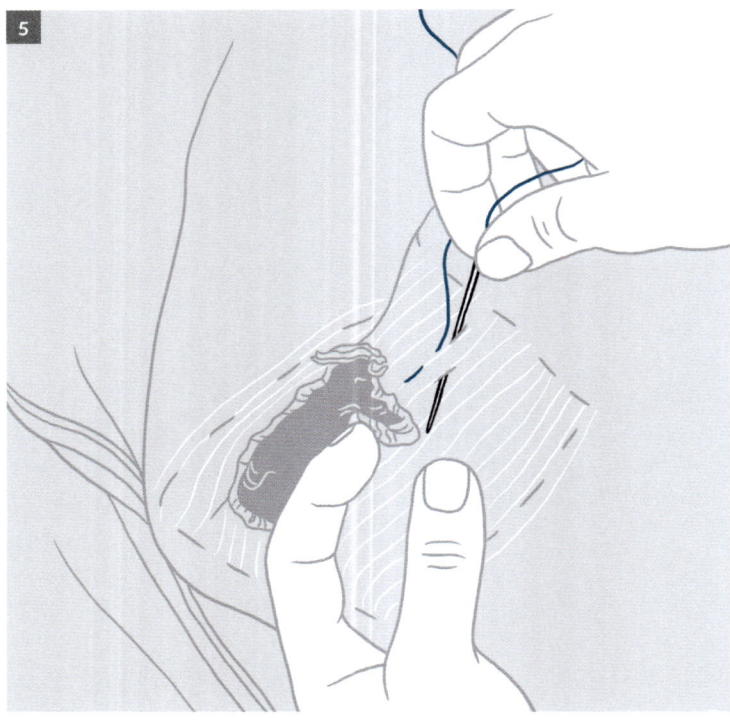

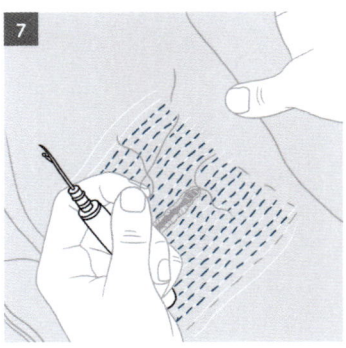

5. As you reach the end of your first row, stop with one more stitch left to make. With the needle on the top of your fabric, pull the thread through to show the stitches you have made – don't pull it too tight. You should have an evenly spaced line of stitches along the grid that you marked out. Push your needle down to make the last stitch and then bring the needle back up at an angle on the next line down; this will bring your needle up in position to work back in the opposite direction to create the next row of stitches. You can choose to mirror the stitches so that they all line up together, or stagger them as I have done here, creating a brick-pattern effect.

6. Don't pull the thread too tightly at the end of each row; instead allow for a small loop of thread in between rows (on the WS of the jeans) to allow the thread to move and stretch with the fabric. It's a good practice to get into to check the tension of your stitching every row or so to make sure that your clothing hasn't puckered in any way.

7. Repeat the steps until you have covered the entire hole and your patch is completely secured in place. When you finish the final row of stitches, pull your needle through and out to the side and turn the jeans inside out. You can now remove the basting stitches and pull the tail threads through to either weave in (see page 35) or knot off. If you choose to knot the threads off, remember to allow for a little slack and don't tie them too tightly.

Back pockets

You will need:
A fabric patch big enough to allow at least a 1-cm (3/8-in) margin all round the hole
A sashiko needle
Sashiko cotton thread
Basting thread and a hand-sewing needle or pins
A thimble
A fabric marker or chalk pencil
A ruler or stitching template

My mend:
Wear and tear to the side of a back pocket, mended using a patch and sashiko crosses

Back pockets are often heavily used and get worn out from hands repeatedly reaching for phones, wallets and keys. The damage tends to occur on the side seams or corner seams of the pockets, and these kinds of tears lend themselves really well to visible repairs as you can use the damage to create a window to the fabric that you choose to patch with underneath, or embellish the whole area with a sashiko stitch pattern. As with all repairs, the key here is to reinforce not just the tear but also the surrounding area of fabric.

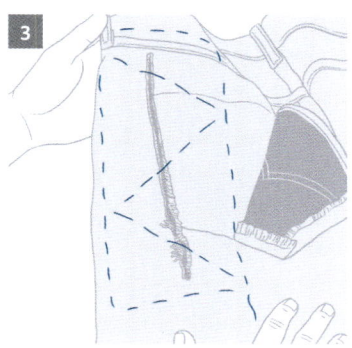 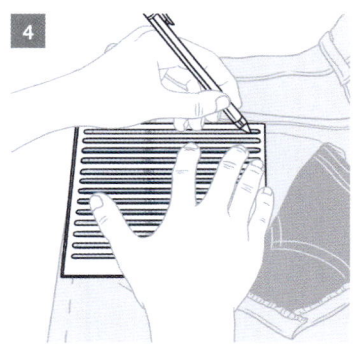

1. Whether the tear is right alongside the back pocket of the jeans or just in the corner, partially removing the pocket before you start stitching will make the whole process a lot easier. Use a seam ripper to unpick the pocket topstitching just enough so that you can access the rip and surrounding fabric, then keep the pocket folded back and out of the way.

2. Turn the jeans inside out (WS) and use sharp scissors to trim away any frayed fabric from the tear.

3. Position your fabric patch with the right side facing down and baste or pin it into place. It's important at this point to make sure that the patch and the jeans are all lying flat and not puckering anywhere. As the rip in this garment spanned the whole height of the pocket, I added a diagonal row of basting stitches running across the centre of the patch as well as all around the edges to make sure that the ripped fabric couldn't move around (shown here from the right side).

4. Turn the jeans back to the right side (RS). As the fabric patch is underneath the rip here, the rip itself is a feature of the repair, but it will still need to be stitched over to add strength. Decide on your sashiko pattern, then use a fabric marker or chalk and a template or ruler to mark out the pattern over both fabric and patch.

NOTE: As my repair used cross stitches, I drew out a 5mm- (¼in-) square grid to create evenly spaced stitches all over. This isn't essential, as organically worked stitches look just as good, but it can be helpful to have these lines to follow, especially when you are working on a larger repair.

5. Thread your needle and begin stitching vertically up and down over the patch, remembering to leave a tail of thread when you start to be woven in at the end. Make sure that you're sewing through both the jeans and the fabric patch underneath. Remember to work all the way out from the centre of the rip to the surrounding fabric area – the more stitches you add, the stronger the repair will be.

NOTE: Even though the patch was basted into place, I still started stitching as close as possible to the rip and then worked subsequent lines moving outwards to ensure that the jeans and the patch fabric remained lying flat while sewing.

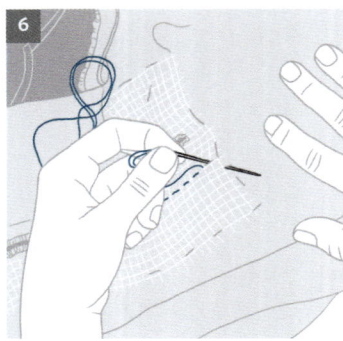

6. At the end of each row, at the final stitch, bring your needle up on the next marker line, ready to start sewing the next row.

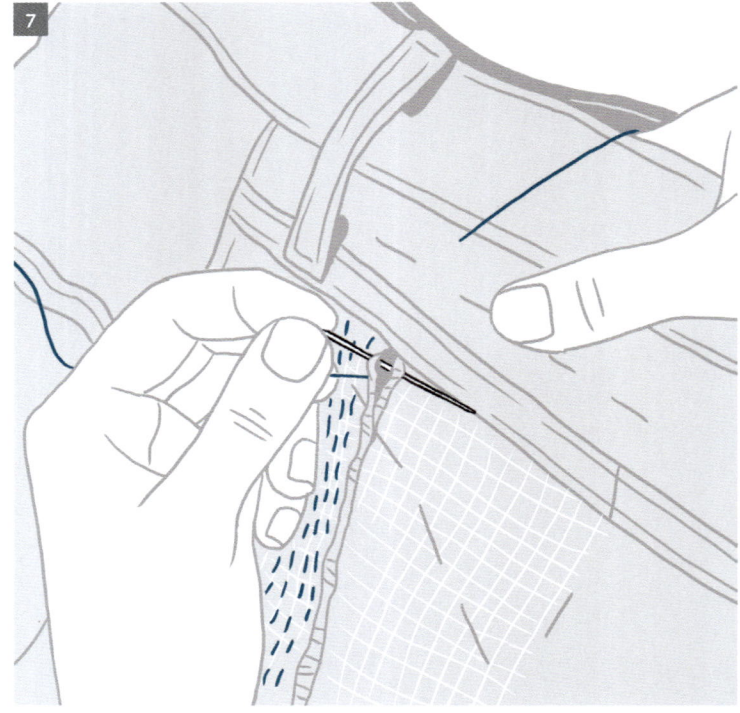

7. Work all the way along the damaged area, securing the patch into place until the whole area is covered in a series of running stitches. Make sure that you are continuing to stitch through both the jeans and the fabric patch underneath, and that you're not pulling the thread too tightly at the end of each row. When you reach the hole, or any area that is too frayed to stitch, skip a row and then continue on the next row where you're able to stitch through the jeans and the fabric patch.

8. Once you've completed all your rows in one direction, it's a good idea to remove the basting stitches (which are no longer needed) and remove the fabric-marker grid; it's easier to use the existing stitches to determine the placement of the horizontal stitches in the next step. This is up to you, though; you may find it better to keep the grid. (I always think it's worth remembering that even with a grid, we are humans not machines. There will always be small variations in our stitches, which should be celebrated!)

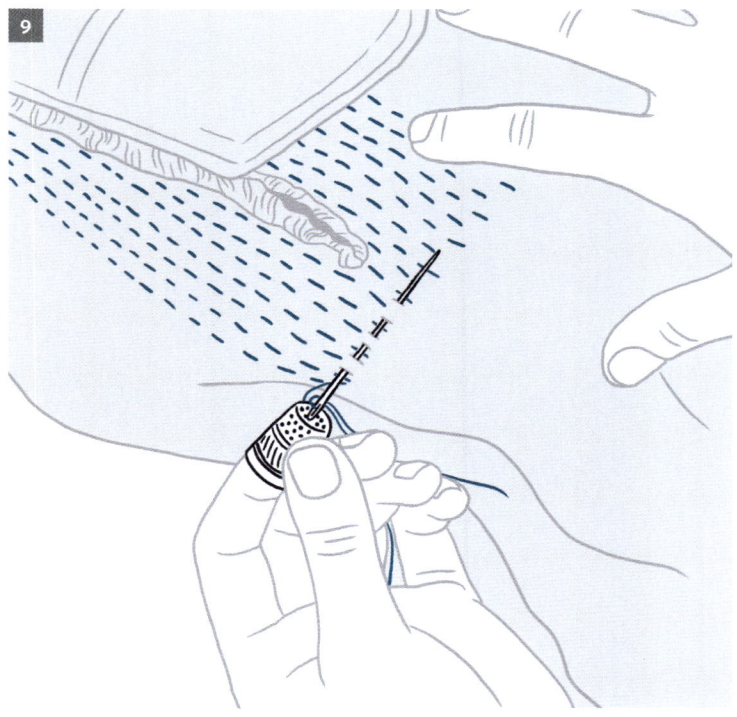
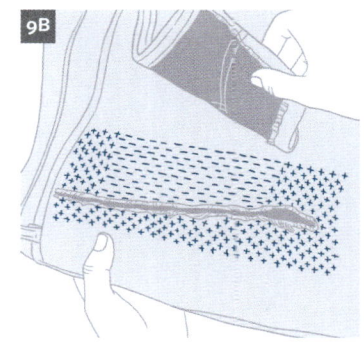

9. Now stitch back across the vertical stitches horizontally to cross them and create a cross pattern across the whole ripped area. You don't need to stitch back across the stitches that will be covered by the pocket once the repair is complete – the vertical stitches keep the patch in place securely enough, and since they won't be seen, the horizontal stitches aren't necessary there.

10. Once you have completed all the horizontal stitches, turn the jeans inside out to trim the patch down, if needed, and weave in the ends (see page 35). I used the stitches on the inside here to weave the tail threads though to keep them flat and secure.

11. The final step is to re-attach the pocket. Put the pocket back into position and follow the shadow of the old stitching to sew it back into place. I used a sewing machine for this, but you can do it by hand; just remember to work one stitch at a time, and use a thimble! I chose to use a thread that matched the original pocket topstitching, but there's no reason that you couldn't extend the visible mending aspect to this step too, by using the sashiko thread.

Belt loops

My mend:
Wear and tear to jean belt loops, which are reattached to a patched area

Pulling your jeans on using the belt loops as leverage seems to have become a very common habit, but often ends with the belt loops breaking or the entire area underneath them ripping. I recommend using a thimble and working one stitch at a time when repairing this kind of damage, as you'll be stitching through several layers of denim, but don't be put off by that, as these small tears can be a great place to get creative with your repairs! Alternatively, if you'd prefer to use a sewing machine, you could instead use the machine-darning technique on page 60 to reinforce the fabric before reattaching the belt loop with topstitching thread that matches the rest of the jeans.

You will need:
A fabric patch big enough to allow at least a 1-cm (3/8-in) margin all round the hole
A sashiko needle
Sashiko cotton thread
Basting thread and a hand-sewing needle or pins
A thimble
A fabric marker or chalk pencil

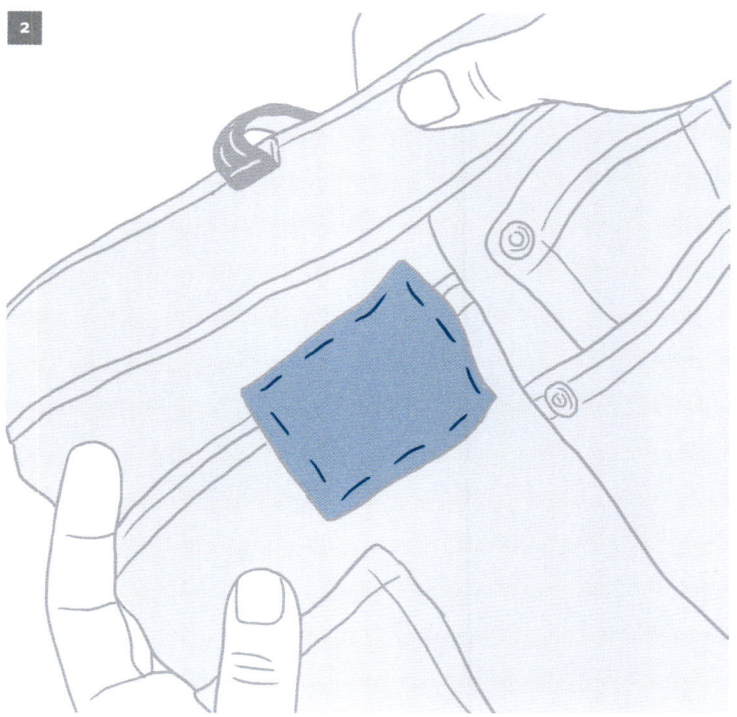

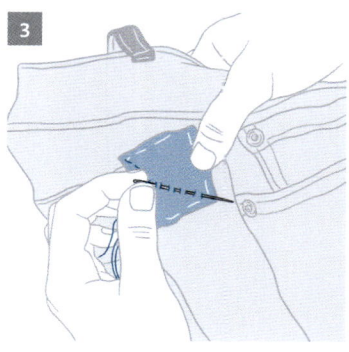

1. If the belt loop is still attached to the jeans and the rip is underneath, use a seam ripper to remove the lower stitching on the loop (leaving it attached at the top) and keep it out of the way for now. Trim off any loose and frayed threads that may interfere with your repair.

2. To reinforce the area, you will need a patch of fabric placed on top of or underneath the area of damage. Rather than hiding my indigo-dyed cotton, I decided to place it on top of the jeans. The edges of the patch have been left raw to avoid adding bulk to the area by folding the edges under. As always, you can choose to pin or baste the patch into place, but I find, especially with smaller patches and thicker fabrics, that basting makes the process a lot easier. It also allows you a little more freedom to experiment with stitching freehand (because you don't have to worry about stitching around pins).

3. For this repair the fabric patch has been stitched into place freehand with straight rows of stitches, rather than using a sashiko template; this approach works well with small patches. Start sewing diagonally from one corner of the patch, picking up several stitches at a time to create a relatively straight row of stitches, just as with the knee patch repair on page 49. Remember to leave a nice long tail. When you reach the end of the row, bring your needle up in position to start the next row, as before.

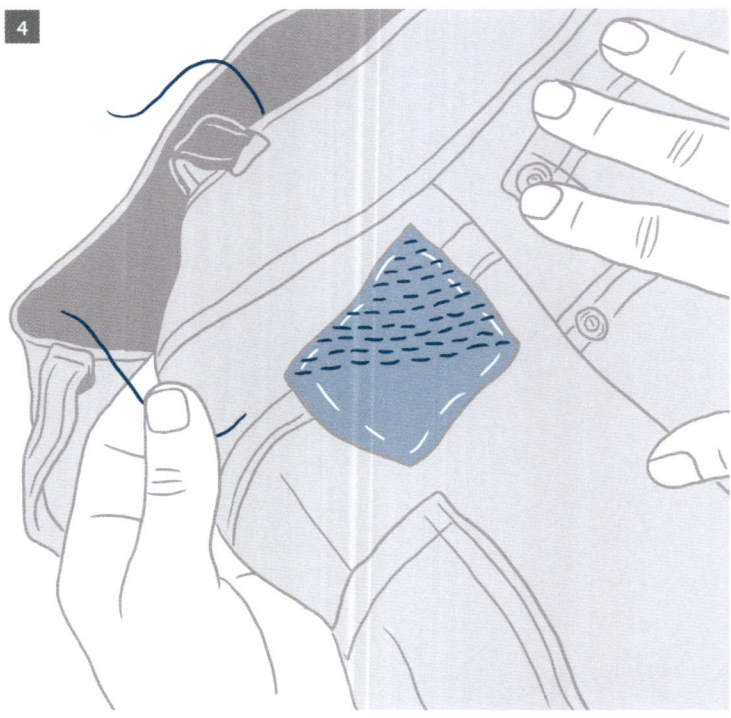

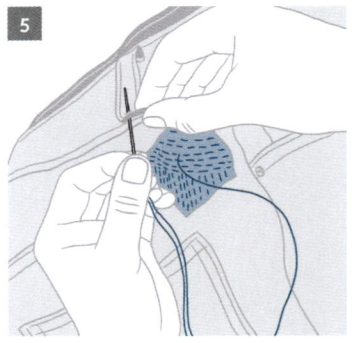

4. Continue back and forth in rows to fill in half of the patch. You can then continue the straight lines of stitching until you have covered the entire fabric patch and damaged area of fabric. Or, as I have done, you can rotate the jeans 90 degrees and sew the remaining lines at right angles to the first set of rows. On your last stitch, bring your needle down and through to the wrong side of your fabric, ready to secure the tail threads.

5. Once the damaged area has been repaired, you can focus on reattaching the belt loop and securing it into place by sewing through the seam allowance (turn under) of the belt loop and the patch fabric underneath using a whip stitch. Working through several layers of denim can be really tough so it's best to tackle these next few stitches one step at a time. With a new length of thread, bring your needle up from the inside (WS) of your jeans through to the right side of the fabric in line with where the belt loop naturally sits. Then bring your belt loop into position and push your needle through and up, just into that seam allowance of the belt loop, as shown.

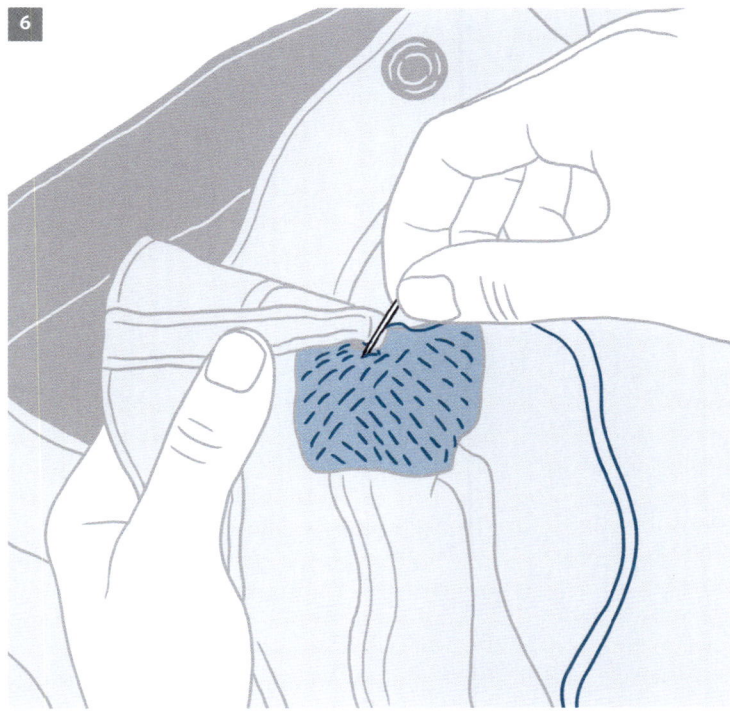

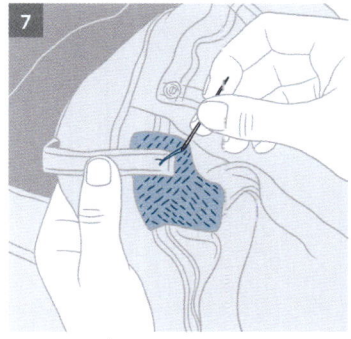

6. Bring your needle back down and through to the wrong side of the jeans, then back up again, ready to go through the belt loop seam allowance. These whip stitches will be fairly invisible once finished.

7. Repeat these steps for one side of the belt loop seam allowance, then repeat on the other side to secure it into place on the jeans. As a final step, you can also add a finishing stitch all the way through the centre of the belt loop at the bottom. Work very slowly and carefully to push your needle all the way through and up the layers of fabric to make either a single stitch or a cross stitch, and remember to use a thimble!

8. To finish, bring your needle and thread down through to the inside (WS) of the jeans and then tie off or weave in the tail threads (see page 35).

Crotch

My mend:
Wear and tear to the inside leg/crotch of denim jeans, repaired using machine darning

You will need:
A fabric patch big enough to allow at least a 1-cm (3/8-in) margin all round the hole/damaged area
A sewing machine with an embroidery or darning foot
Machine sewing thread in two colours
Basting thread and a hand-sewing needle or pins

Damage to the crotch of jeans is so common! For this kind of repair I recommend using a sewing machine for machine darning, as it is super strong and adds minimal bulk to the jeans. Choosing a thread colour that closely matches your jeans will result in a very subtle repair but, having said that, if you choose to use a contrasting thread colour it will add a great texture and tactile quality to the denim and won't be as visible when worn as you'd think.

Machine darning can be tricky to get used to, and I recommend using a specific darning or embroidery/free-motion foot for the best results. It also helps to practice on any denim scraps you have, to get comfortable with the amount of movement required for evenly spaced stitches on different fabrics, as this will vary depending on the type of denim you are repairing, and how much Lycra or stretch there is in the jeans. With a machine darning foot, you will also need to drop the feed dogs (the toothed tracks that show through your sewing machine plate and move your fabric along while sewing) and I find that it's best to remove the arm of the sewing machine so that you can insert the jeans more easily.

The main thing to remember is to run your stitches in line with the direction of the denim for an almost invisible repair; the twill weave of denim fabric gives a diagonal effect, and when you follow these diagonal lines with your stitches, you'll see they blend almost seamlessly into the fabric. As an extra step, you could also stitch back across those first stitches at a 180-degree angle to create a web of stitching for even further reinforcement.

NOTE: If you don't have access to a sewing machine, you can also use the repair methods shown for the main body, knees and back pockets (pages 44, 48, 52) for crotch repairs. Repairing by hand is still a great option, but remember to consider the weight and bulk that will be created by using fabric patches and sashiko thread, in comparison to finer machine thread.

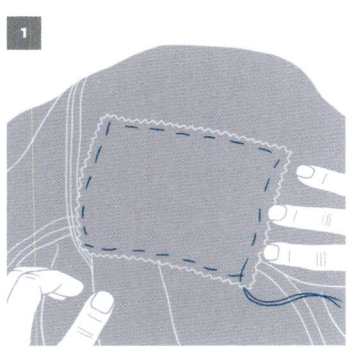 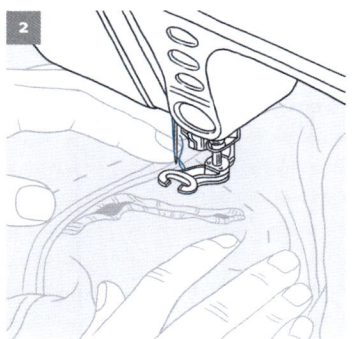 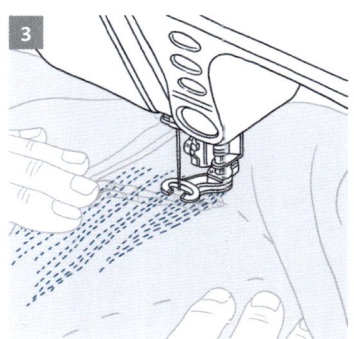

1. Turn the jeans inside out (WS). Baste your fabric patch in position on the inside (WS) of the jeans in the same way as any other patch repair method, remembering to place the patch correctly so that the fabric stretches in the same direction as the jeans and is facing right-side down.

2. Turn the jeans right side out (RS) and – with a darning/embroidery foot attached to your sewing machine, the feed dogs down, and a straight stitch length of 2–2.5mm (approx. 1/12in) – place the jeans under the machine and start sewing lines of stitches up and down over the hole, following the diagonal lines of the fabric. Remember to sew a few backstitches at the start and end. Note that, despite having a stitch length set, because the feed dogs have been dropped you will be able to manoeuvre the fabric as you sew, so your stitch length may vary. I tend to work the first lines of stitches fairly close together over the hole itself, before going back across to add a wider series of stitches around the whole area to help blend the repair in.

3. Try to aim for what looks essentially like densely worked lines of stitches in a long zig-zag formation. Work slowly to make sure you're creating even stitch lengths, and that your jeans aren't being stretched or pulled out of shape in the process.

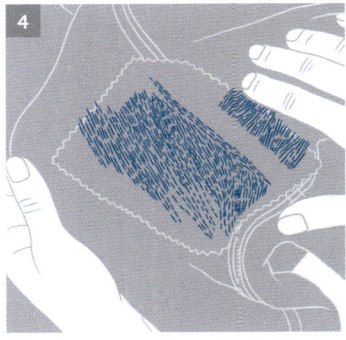

4. When the patch is secure, you can remove the basting stitches before turning the jeans around and reinforcing the stitches further with a crosshatch effect if needed. Once you have finished sewing, turn the jeans back inside out (WS) and cut off any loose tail threads. You can also trim down the fabric patch if any of the edges have been left unstitched.

2 *Jumpers & knitwear*

Knitwear seems to stick around in people's wardrobes for much longer than other garments. Whereas jeans and T-shirts can be worn throughout the year, jumpers and knits tend to be stored away for several months before keeping us wrapped up warm all through winter. We also tend to opt for looser-fitting jumpers and cardigans to allow for layering, which means they're more likely to stay with us over the years through weight fluctuations and style changes. This reduced wear doesn't necessarily protect your knits, though, as moths can cause havoc, especially on wool and cashmere in storage. If made from natural fibres, knitwear often wears out more quickly and can be snagged easily, leading to holes and laddering. Luckily, there are lots of great darning techniques that can be used and applied according to the type of knit and area of damage.

Ladders

You will need:
A latch hook or a crochet hook in a size that best matches the thickness of the clothing
Yarn in a similar weight to the clothing
A tapestry needle

Ladders in knitted fabrics are very common, and often travel down from a hole in the fabric, so it's best to start by fixing them before moving on to repairing the hole. The ladders are caused by dropped stitches that can spread quickly up and down your knits, but luckily they are also very easy to knit back into place.

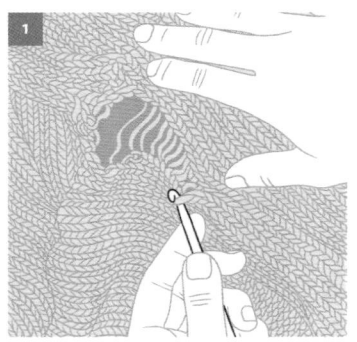

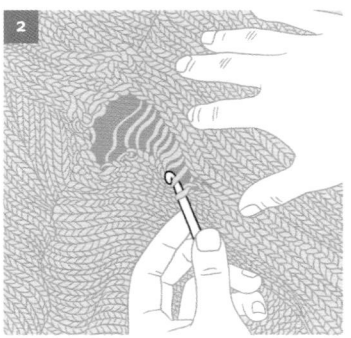

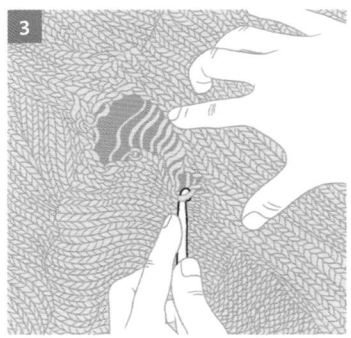

1. Find the bottom of the ladder and pick up the first available dropped stitch on to your latch hook or crochet hook.

2. Insert your hook underneath the next dropped stitch above to pick it up. A latch hook will make this really easy, as it has a small arm that catches the second stitch while releasing the first, but you can angle your crochet hook and use your fingers if needed to pull the first stitch over and off.

3. Pull this stitch under the first stitch, interlocking them as the first stitch falls off the hook. You should now be left with one stitch on your hook (the second stitch you picked up) while the first is back in its original position in the fabric underneath.

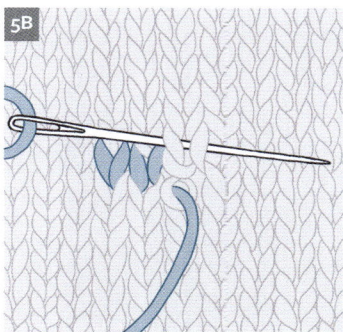
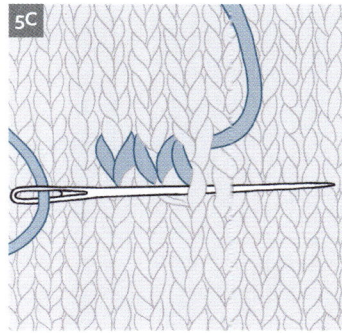

4. Repeat this process all the way up the ladder. If there is still a hole at the top of the ladder you can use a needle and thread to secure the last stitch to its neighbouring stitch, then darn over the hole with your chosen technique.

5. If you can completely close up the hole by picking up the dropped stitches, when you reach the top you can secure the final loop into place with Swiss darning (see page 24). To do this, thread up a needle with a matching weight yarn (and colour, if you want an invisible finish here!) and make a few duplicate stitches on the row above and to one side of the remaining loop.
As you approach the final loop, pick it up with your needle and continue along the row for a few more stitches to secure it into place.

6. Finally, push your needle through to the inside of the clothing (WS) and weave in the tail thread.

Elbows

My mend:
Wear and tear to a worn-through elbow, mended using Scotch darning

You will need:
Yarn of a similar weight and matching fibre content to the clothing
A darning or tapestry needle that matches the weight of your chosen yarn
A darning mushroom and elastic tie or hairband

You might notice on well-worn jumpers that one elbow tends to wear out before the other because of the way you sit or work, and the Scotch darning technique (see page 27) works really well to repair these holes. It uses the blanket-stitch technique worked in rows to create a strong, square patch. I love the tactile finish of it, especially when used on more unusual knit patterns.

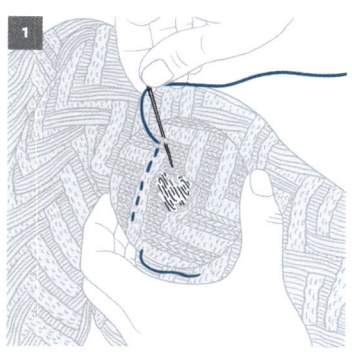 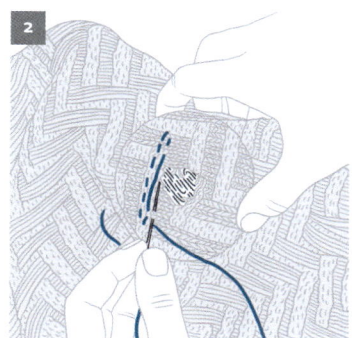 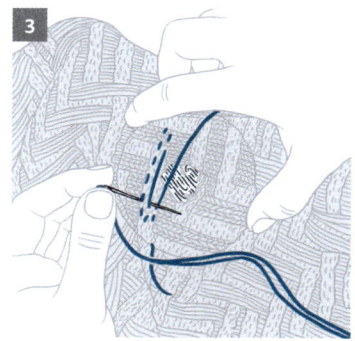

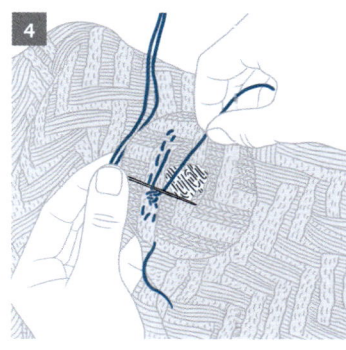

1. To start, place a darning mushroom or disc underneath the hole on the inside (WS) of your clothing and hold it in place with an elastic band or hairband. Insert your needle from the edge of the mushroom and bring it up into position above the hole. Make a row of running stitches above the area to be repaired, at least 1cm (3/8in) away from the hole, and when making the last stitch position your needle down and back up again below this first row ready to start the next row. For an evenly filled repair, the distance between each row needs to be about the width of the yarn that you are using.

2. On the second row, do a single running stitch, then create one long weft stitch over the hole, securing it into place at the other side of the hole with another running stitch. Create one more running stitch underneath this to start a third row, and now you are ready to start creating the Scotch darn. (You can add as many running stitches to the sides of these long weft stitches as you like.)

3. Insert your needle underneath one of the stitches that you made on the first row and also underneath the long weft stitch that you made in row two.

4. Pull your needle through, making sure the working thread is in position under your needle – as you pull the needle and thread through this will catch it and create your first stitch.

5. Repeat this process along your first row of stitches and the weft stitch, remembering to insert the needle underneath both rows of stitches and thread, and ensuring that you catch your working thread as you pull the stitches through. When you reach the end of the long weft stitch, insert your needle to the side and pull through to secure this first row into place. Create one more running stitch and, as before, move your needle down and into position to start the row below.

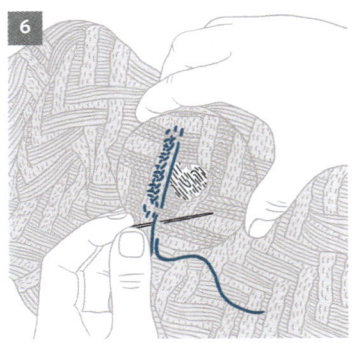 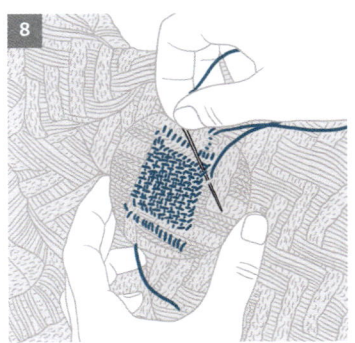 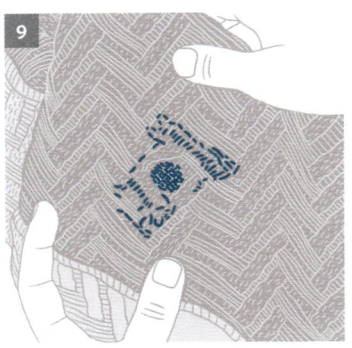

6. Create another long weft stitch and running stitch back to the other side, then move your needle down into position to start working the blanket stitch again. You will need to create this weft row each time before you can start making the next row of stitches.

7. Now that you have a row of Scotch darn stitches to work with, rather than the initial running stitches from the top row, insert your needle underneath the previous row of stitches as well as the new weft stitch to start working the stitches again, in the same way.

8. Repeat these steps until you have covered the whole area of damage. For the final row, you'll need to secure the previous row of stitches to the clothing. To do this, insert your needle down and underneath the previous row of stitches as before, but then you will pick up a single stitch of the clothing underneath as well and pull the needle through both. You do not need to create a long weft row to do this, just work across the last row you worked. Repeat this all the way along your last row of stitches until the patch is secured to the clothing.

9. When you reach the other side, create one last running stitch and then push your needle out to the edge of the darning mushroom and through. You can now remove the darning mushroom and pull your tail threads through to the inside to weave in and finish.

JUMPERS & KNITWEAR

Main body

Swiss darning can be a fiddly technique to get to grips with, but is really simple once you get accustomed to recreating the original stockinette stitches. The main thing to remember is to regularly check the tension of your stitches and how they are lying against the rest of the surrounding stitches and fabric. If you use a matching-coloured yarn to work an invisible repair, this technique will blend in seamlessly.

This green cardigan was a patchwork of moth holes, and while Swiss darning worked well for some smaller areas, I used standard darning to cover the larger holes. If working with fine and 'fuzzy' knits such as mohair, Swiss darning can be very time consuming, so keep this in mind when choosing where to use it.

My mend:
A hole in the front body of a cardigan, closed up using Swiss darning

You will need:
Yarn of a similar weight and matching fibre content to the clothing
A tapestry or ball-tipped darning needle to match the weight of the yarn
A tailor's ham, soft pincushion or sponge
Pins or a needle and thread to create grafting stitches

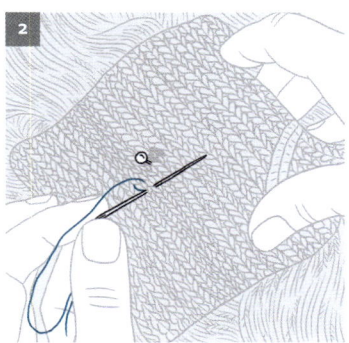 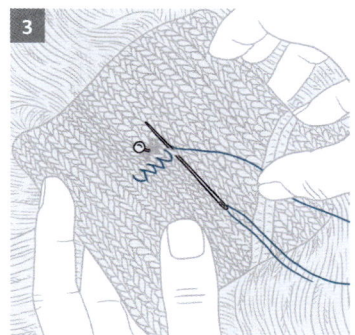 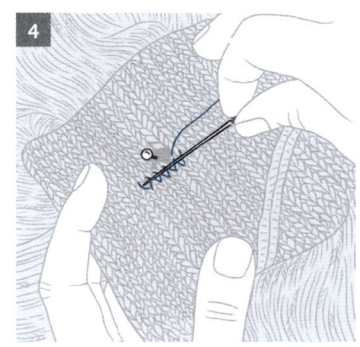

1. To start, trim any loose threads and place a pincushion, tailor's ham or sponge underneath the hole. Catch any loops that you can see in the hole, using pins to hold them in place. Push your needle down through the fabric a little way from the hole and then up into position at the bottom point of one V stitch a few rows below the hole.

2. Follow that V stitch thread up and around to where it loops behind the V in the row above – inserting your needle, follow the same path to make a stitch of your own. When you pull your needle and thread through, this will create one half of a V stitch. Bring your needle back down into the first stitch (the bottom point of the V), ready to move across horizontally in order to start the next stitch. (Note: these illustrations show a fine mending thread for clarity, but your yarn will 'cover' the original stitches of the garment. See page 65, step 5, for detailed illustrations showing this technique.)

3. Continue along the row in this way to build up a series of new V stitches until you are ready to move up to the next row. To do this, instead of moving your needle across to the next stitch horizontally, go down into the point of the V stitch you're making and then bring the needle under the horizontal loop of thread above and up into position at the point of the V on the row above.

4. You'll then work back across the next row in the opposite direction to the first, picking up the stitches from the row you have just made. (You are essentially replicating, or sewing over, the existing knit stitch.)

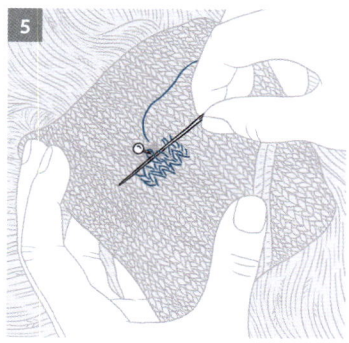

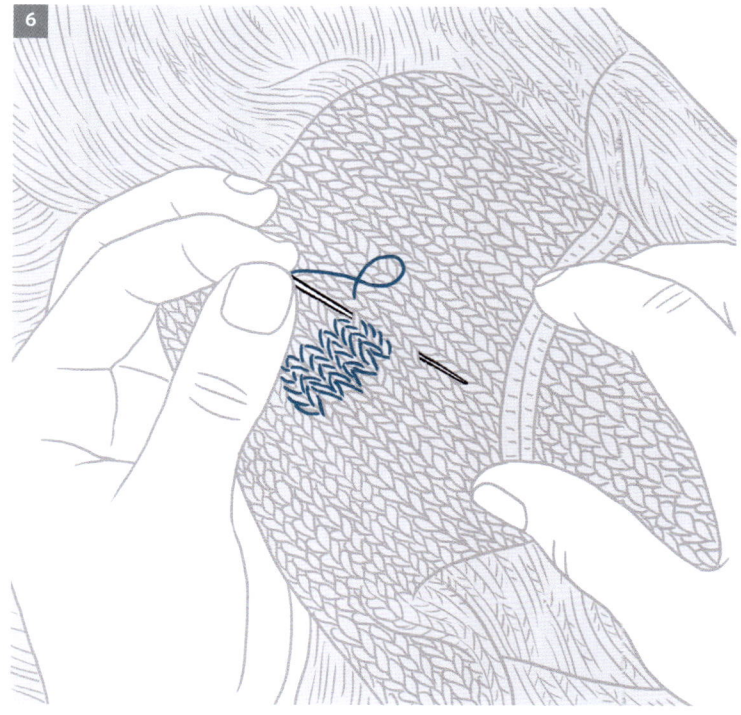

5. As you approach the hole and the pins holding the existing knit loops, put more pins into position on the next row up to act as placeholders to loop your thread around for the new stitches. Check the existing rows and columns of stitches around the hole to work out how many new stitches (and therefore pins) you'll need. You can remove the pins as you work once the new stitches have been secured by the next row. Creating new even stitches over the hole can be tricky, and this is where I find the pins useful, as they help create a consistent tension and loop size as you work, as well as acting as a clear indicator of how many stitches you need to make per row.

6. Once the hole has been covered, continue stitching a few more rows above in the same way to reinforce the existing yarn. Then bring your needle and thread out to the side of the darn.

7. Pull the tail threads through to the inside of the clothing to weave in.

MAIN BODY 73

Underarms

Darning from the back, or inside, of your clothing allows the shape of the hole to become a frame for the repair on the front, rather than covering it up completely with darning from the front. This can be a really creative way to show off your darn and the shape of the hole you've repaired, and is a very traditional method of darning that would have been used with matching yarns to create a more discreet repair.

Both this repair and the cuffs and hems repairs (see pages 78–83) have been created using 100 percent cotton DK yarn that I doubled up to match the weight of the cotton jumper. However, you can of course use a single yarn that matches the weight of the fabric. I wanted to show an example of how easy it is to do this if you're ever stuck trying to find exactly the right thread weight for your clothing. Doubling up the yarn also creates a really textured basket-weave effect, which I personally really like. You could even use two different yarn colours at the same time for a variegated finish.

My mend:
A hole in the underarm of a chunky knit, darned from the back

You will need:
Yarn of a similar weight (either single-stranded or doubled up) and matching fibre content to the clothing
A darning needle to match the weight of the yarn
A darning mushroom and tie

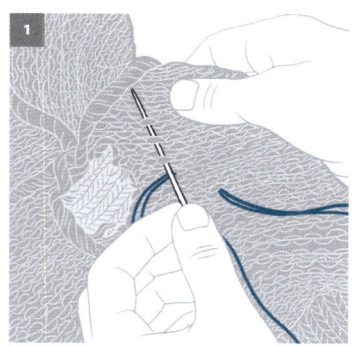
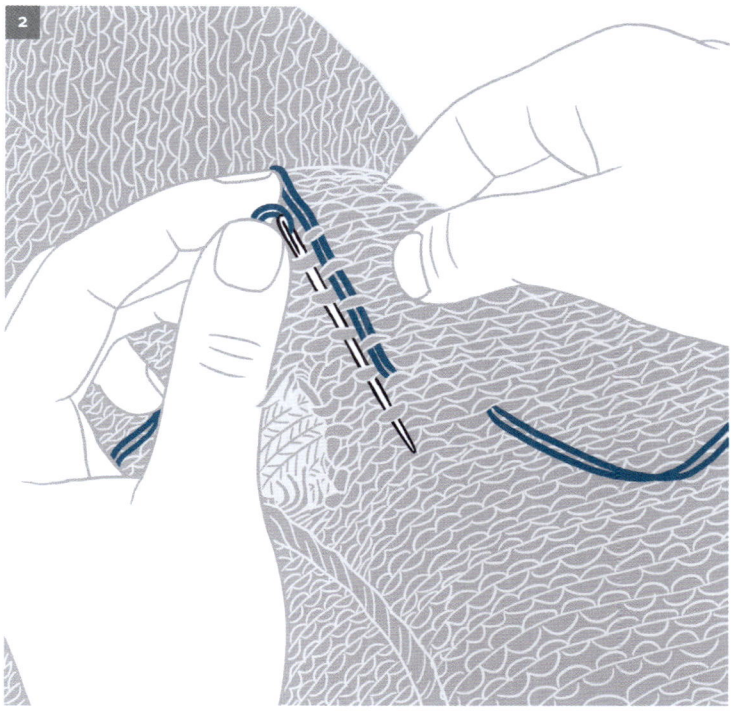

1. On the inside (WS) of the fabric, place a darning mushroom or disc underneath the hole and hold in place, if needed, with an elastic tie. The hole on this jumper was too big to use a darning mushroom, so I worked freehand very carefully, checking every few rows to make sure that the tension was right. To start with, you'll create a few rows of vertical running stitches alongside the hole to add strength, before creating the warp threads. With a darning needle threaded up, bring your needle up and into position at least 1cm (³⁄₈in) away from the hole. Remember to leave a tail of thread to be woven in at the end. Begin picking up every other weft stitch in the garment to create a row of running stitches.

2. When you reach the top, move your needle over to the next series of existing weft stitches ready to create your second row. Try to alternate the weft stitches that you pick up with each row so that you build up a brickwork pattern of stitches. Don't pull the stitches too tightly – allow a small loop or slack of thread at the end of each row on the inside. Make sure the distance between the rows is around the width of your thread to ensure an evenly filled darn.

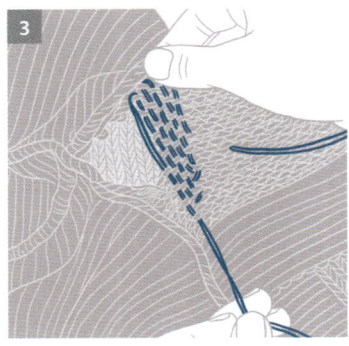

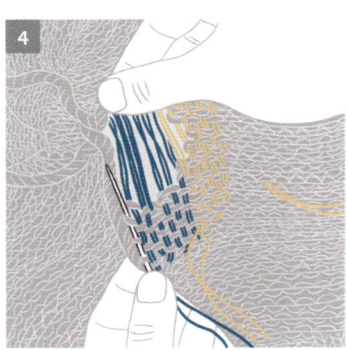

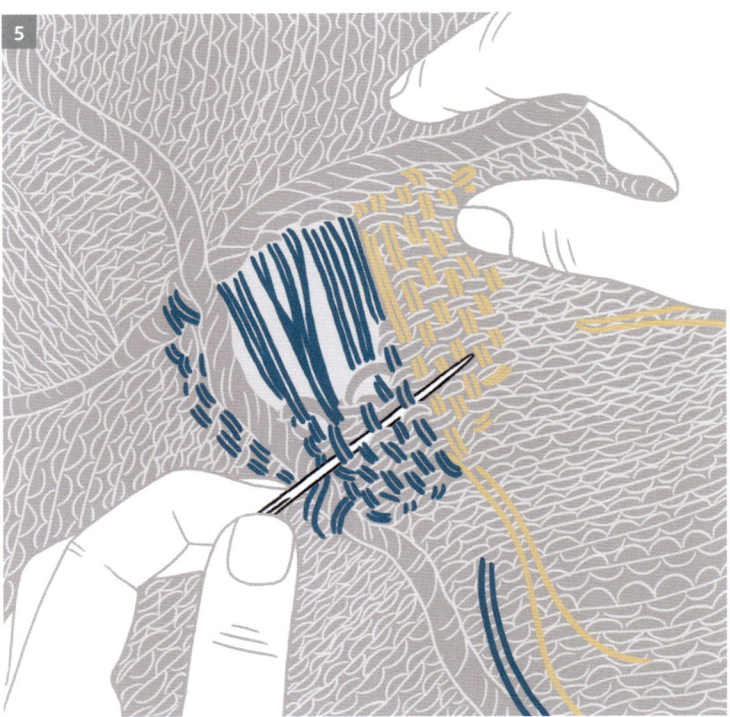

3. When you reach the hole, create long warp stitches to cover the area, then secure with a few more running stitches; if there are any loops of the knit fabric at the edges of the hole, you can catch these with the needle when creating the warp rows.

4. Continue in this way until you have covered the area to darn. As this hole was right against two seams, I worked as closely as I could to the seams and then extended the darn over on the other side of the seam as well. I also chose to change colours periodically as I worked to build up a checked pattern for the finished darn (in the illustration, the new active thread is highlighted blue). This isn't essential at all but can be a fun way to create more colourful darns – just remember there will be more ends to weave in if you do this.

5. To start your horizontal weft rows, use a new piece of thread and bring your needle in from the side as before, coming up underneath the hole. Start a series of running stitches that weave under and over the stitches you made next to the hole until your needle arrives at the bottom of the long warp threads.

JUMPERS & KNITWEAR   76

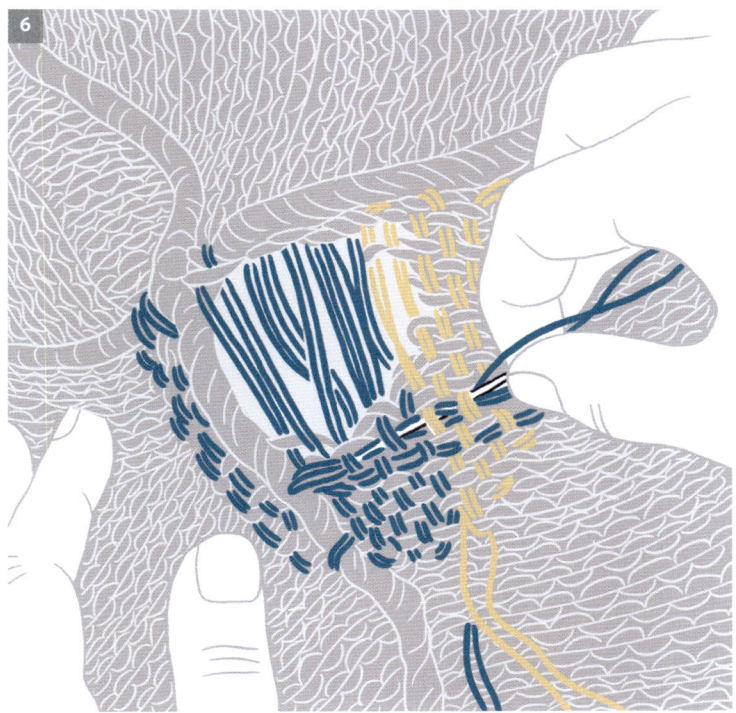

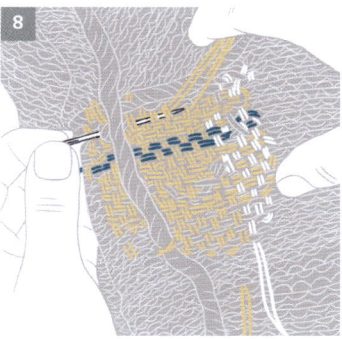

8. Continue as before, weaving over and under the warp threads over the hole and the other side. Repeat these steps until you have filled your warp threads. Occasionally use the needle to push down your rows as you work to fill any gaps and keep the patch nice and even.

6. Continue your row of stitching over the long warp threads you created earlier by weaving the needle alternately over and under the warp threads: over one, under one and so on. If you're not using a tapestry or blunt-tip needle, turn your needle around so that you are using the eye of the needle to do the weaving.

7. Repeat until you reach the end of the warp threads, then continue weaving over and under the running stitches on the other side. When you're ready to start the next row, bring your needle up into position on the next row and go back in the opposite direction. Repeat the previous steps to weave back across your warp threads, changing the order in which you go over and under the threads – if you went over a warp thread on the first row, for this row you will go under it.

9. Continue until you have woven the needle under and over all your warp threads. When you reach the end, finish the final series of running stitches and then bring your needle out at the edge of your darn. Weave in all the tail threads on the wrong side (WS) of the fabric.

Cuffs & hems

You will need:
Yarn of a similar weight and matching fibre content to the clothing
A darning needle that matches the weight of the yarn
A jam jar or tailor's ham to mimic the shape of the sleeve

My mend:
A torn and frayed cuff, reconstructed using plain-weave darning

Repairing cuffs with darning requires precision when it comes to the tension of the darned patch. With a standard woven darn, you have the surrounding fabric on every side to maintain even warp and weft threads, but with cuffs and edges, you need to be able to weave your warp threads around and back again to create a new edge for the cuff. It's easy to pull the threads too tightly, which will lead to a puckered darn, or to pull the existing cuff fabric out of shape, leaving you with a distorted and rippled darn.

Working slowly is key, but it makes a big difference to use a sleeve-shaped darning aid to help you keep the cuff edges in shape. You could use an empty jam jar as I have, a tailor's ham or a tightly rolled piece of fabric (just make sure to pick a contrasting colour so you don't accidentally stitch through it!).

To help keep the natural stretch and elasticity of the existing cuff, working several small stitches before the start of each weft row works really well here. With a standard woven darn you create the warp threads first, but weft threads are worked first in this instance to act as a ladder to start connecting the cuff edges back together.

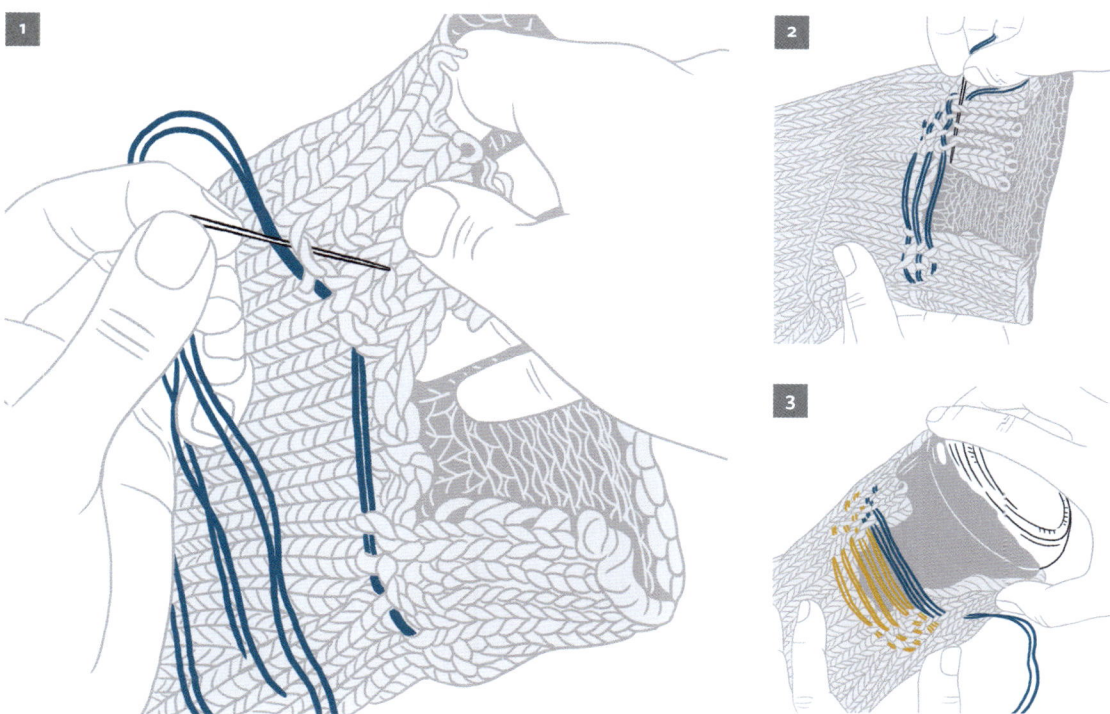

1. If there are any frayed or loose threads around the damaged cuff, trim these back so that you are just left with remaining loops. These can be caught in with your needle and thread as you start to darn.

Starting a few centimetres away from the damage furthest away from the cuff edge, stitch a few small running stitches before creating the first long weft thread, which should be about the same length as the area of damage. Secure it into place with a few more running stitches in the same direction. With your last stitch, angle your needle so that you can bring it up into position ready to start the second weft row, as shown.

2. Keep working in this way, filling over the hole with weft threads, and keeping a close eye on the tension between every row. Make sure that the weft threads and stitches are all lying flat and even and that the shape of the cuff hasn't been distorted (I used my jam jar here to aid the process.) Your weft threads may vary in length, depending on the size and shape of the damaged area.

3. I changed thread colour as I worked, which is reflected in the illustration. Overleaf, the 'active' thread is always blue.

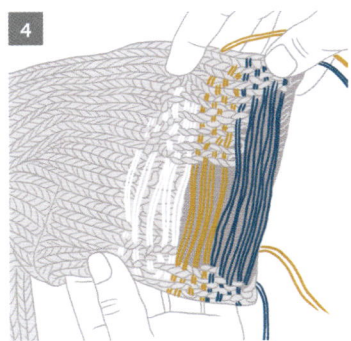

4. When you reach the edge of the cuff, make your final weft row in line with the natural edge of the cuff, again checking the tension carefully.

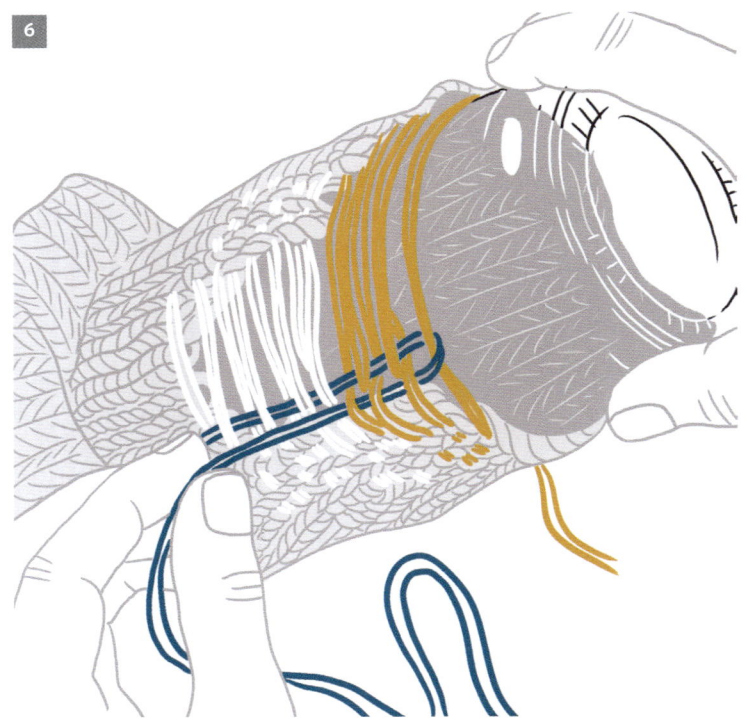

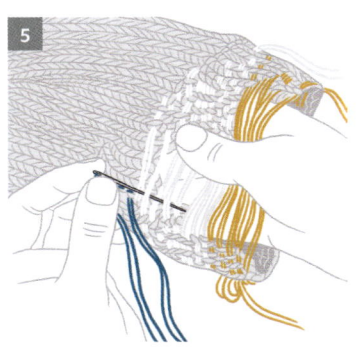

5. Make a few running stitches at the top of the cuff above the centre of the damaged area, then start weaving your first warp row. It can really help with tension to start weaving the warp threads from the centre of the weft threads.

6. When you get to where the edge of the cuff would have been, take the thread either under or over the last weft thread (depending on whether you went over or under the previous weft thread) and then start working back in the opposite direction to create the second warp row, making sure you start with the alternate weave (under if your last one was over, and vice versa). This is where it is crucial to not pull your threads too tightly and to ensure that the darn is lying flat and not too taut, as you are recreating the cuff edge.

JUMPERS & KNITWEAR 80

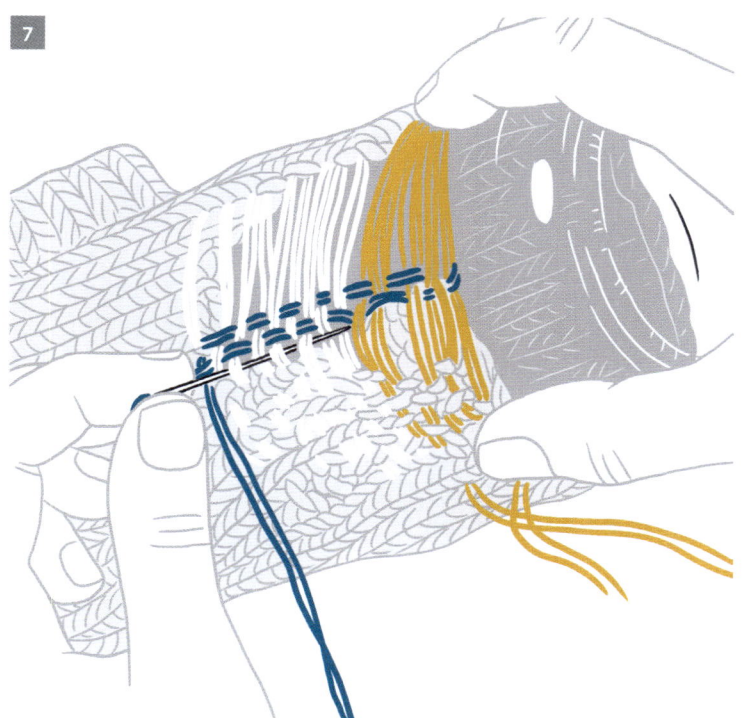

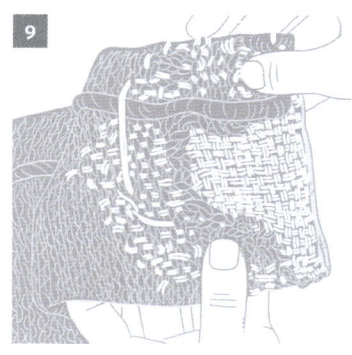

9. Once you have finished weaving in the remaining side, you can remove the jam jar or tailor's ham from the inside of the cuff and turn the whole sleeve inside out. Tackle each trailing tail thread one at a time and weave in the ends in the same way as with a standard darn (see page 35).

7. Continue working from the centre out to fill in one side of the darn, remembering to alternate your over and under stitches on every warp row. As with all darns (and repairs in general!) it's super important to keep checking the natural shape and stretch of your clothing as you are working. It can be easy to get lost in the mending – and that's a great thing! – but for the integrity and longevity of the mend, it really is worth getting into the habit of checking the tension every few rows.

8. Once you have finished one side of the darn, you can start back again at the centre to fill in the other side of the weft threads, repeating steps 5–7.

CUFFS & HEMS 81

Cuffs & hems: fine-knit variation

My mend:
Plain-weave darning on the worn-out cuff of a fine-knit jumper

You will need:
Yarn of a similar weight and matching fibre content to the clothing
A darning needle or ball-tipped needle to match the weight of the yarn
A jar, tailor's ham, darning mushroom or similar

NOTE: If you need to build up a series of darns around the cuff, you can essentially ignore each previous patch when it comes to starting the next. If you need to sew into those running stitches or a little of the darn itself to start building up the next patch, don't worry.

Hoodies and fine-knit jumpers have a tendency to fray quickly and collect small holes on the cuffs and hems. Finished with a double-layered, fold-over ribbed edge, these folds are often the first places to start wearing out and can be tricky to repair in a way that doesn't further stretch the cuff and lose its shape. The previous pages and techniques can still be applied here – you'll just need to shrink down the scale you're working to and select a much finer thread and also a blunt or ball-tipped needle that is fine enough to allow you to work through the ribbed fabric without further damaging the weakened areas.

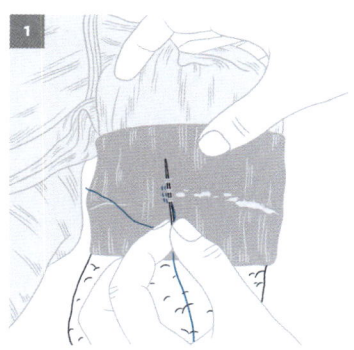 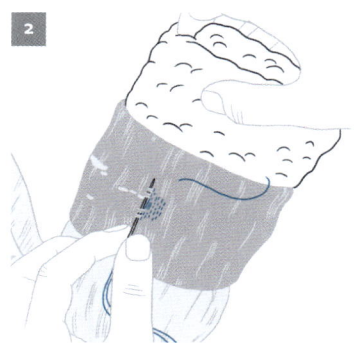 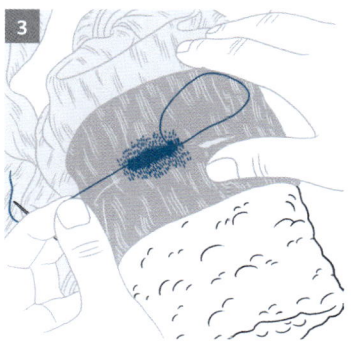

1. One tip I have learned over time is to start by folding double-thickness cuffs like this back and almost in on themselves, so that the crease of the cuff edge is running down the middle of the mend. This allows you to centre the edge of the cuff and the damage as you work, and in my experience means there is less chance of stretching the cuff out of shape. However, it does mean that you can only stitch through one layer of the cuff, which can be a little fiddly. Also, as you need to stitch through just one layer of the cuff, this means that you won't be able to see the inside of the cuff to weave in any tail threads. To deal with this, use the weaving-in method used in sashiko (see page 35) to sew a few stitches in the wrong direction before working back across them in the right direction over the first stitches. This creates a backstitch to secure the thread ends in place.

2. Create a series of running stitches and warp threads as you would with a standard darn (see page 24–5 and 74–7). I find that surrounding any small darned patch with lots of running stitches helps to embed the patch into the cuff, and also helps to keep the right amount of tension and stretch when working on finer knits.

3. When it comes to weaving in the weft threads, you can 'bury' the tail thread in between the layers of the cuff as you bring your needle and thread into position at one side of the warp threads. Fill in your warp threads by weaving over and under each warp thread, securing the thread at the end of every row before moving up to the next.

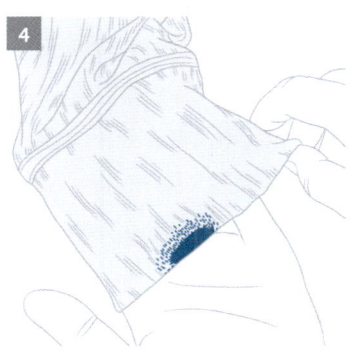

4. When you've filled in all the warp threads, push your needle out to the side between the cuff layers, burying the tail thread before trimming off the excess. Fold the cuff back into its original position; you should now be able to see half of the darn from both sides.

CUFFS & HEMS: FINE-KNIT VARIATION

3 *Shirts*

Although I've focused on shirts in this chapter, any woven item of clothing can be repaired using these techniques. The most common culprits for damage on woven garments are around the seams or areas where a lot of movement is required, such as underarms, cuffs or collars. While strong, woven fabrics don't stretch in the same way as knitted garments, these problem areas can be prone to large rips or tears rather than just being worn down over time.
It's still possible to repair them, though, and it's a great opportunity to reinforce the area against further damage with a range of creative stitches and patches.

Plackets

You will need:
A fabric patch big enough to allow at least a 1-cm (3/8-in) margin all round the hole
A sashiko needle
Sashiko cotton thread or embroidery thread
Basting thread and hand-sewing needle or pins
An iron

My mend:
Wear and tear to a shirt-sleeve placket, mended with whip stitch and a patch

With damage to plackets or on other small seams on a shirt, it is often possible to simply stitch the area back together using either ladder or whip stitch for an invisible finish. However, if there has been some stress to the surrounding fabric, then a patch of fabric underneath can add extra strength – and now is the time to add it.

For this repair, a simple embellishment will work to hold the fabric patch in place and add a subtle visible repair to the area. You can create a geometric series of stitches by working around the seams of the placket, or work organically to create any shapes or patterns you like. On this shirt, I've used a simple whip stitch to secure the patch into place around the edges of the patch on the wrong side, and then around the hole on the right side.

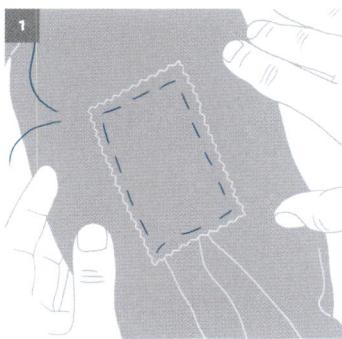

1. With the shirt sleeve turned inside out (WS), baste the fabric patch into place with the right side facing down.

NOTE: When using fabric patches to repair a hole, you can choose to leave the frayed edges of the hole as they are as a feature of the repair, or you can fold them under for a neater finish. When folding the edges under, make sure to trim any excess fraying or loose threads first. I find it easiest to fold the edges under as I am basting the patch into place, but if you prefer you can baste the edges into place at the same time as basting the edges of the patch into position, as shown on page 33.

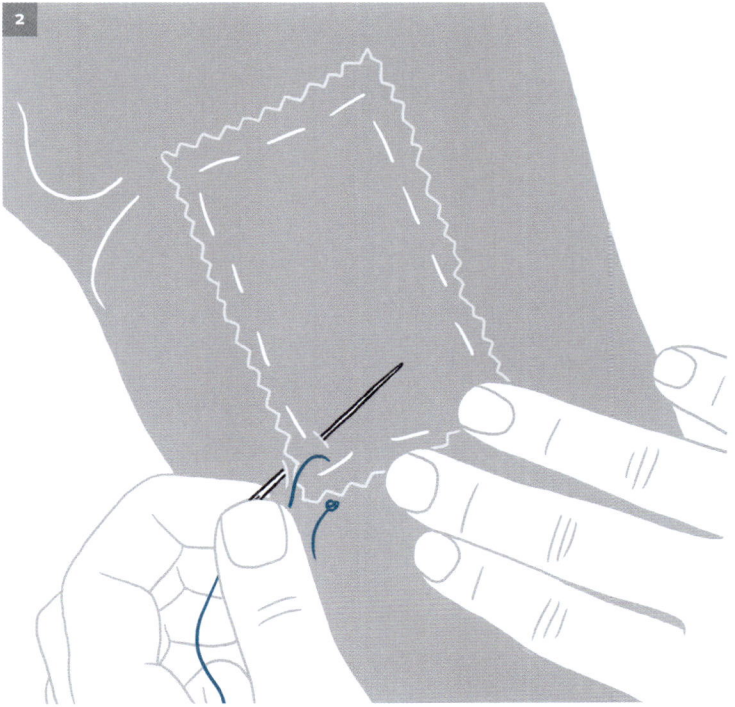

2. Thread your needle and tie a knot in the end, then push your needle and thread up through the patch at one corner, bringing it up on top of the patch ready to start sewing. Push your needle down at the edge of the fabric patch and through the shirt fabric, angling the needle to bring it straight back up again at the side of the first stitch – 5mm to 1cm (¼–⅜ in) is a good distance.

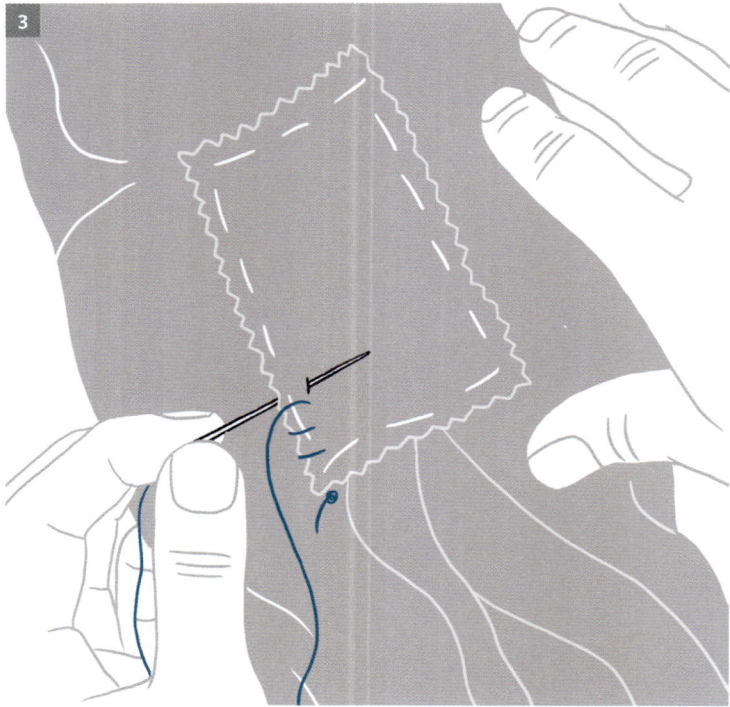

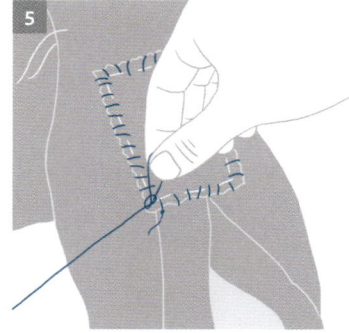

3. Pull your needle and thread through to show this first stitch, then repeat step 2 all the way along the first edge of the fabric patch, making sure to sew through both layers of fabric. Working on the inside (WS) creates stitches that look straight on the inside of the shirt, but will have a diagonal whip stitch finish on the right side; it's basically working whip stitch back to front!

4. When you reach the next corner of the fabric patch, aim to make one more evenly spaced stitch before you bring your needle up and out along the next edge, leaving the same gap between stitches.

5. Continue working in this way all the way around the patch until you reach the place you started, then pull your thread through to the underside of the patch as you did at the beginning, cut off the thread and knot it off (see page 35). Remove the basting stitches from the edge of the patch.

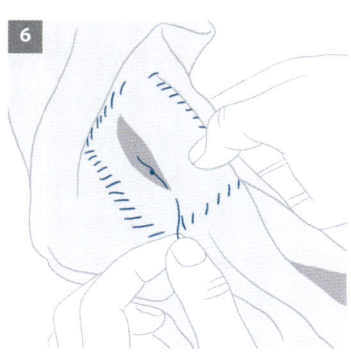

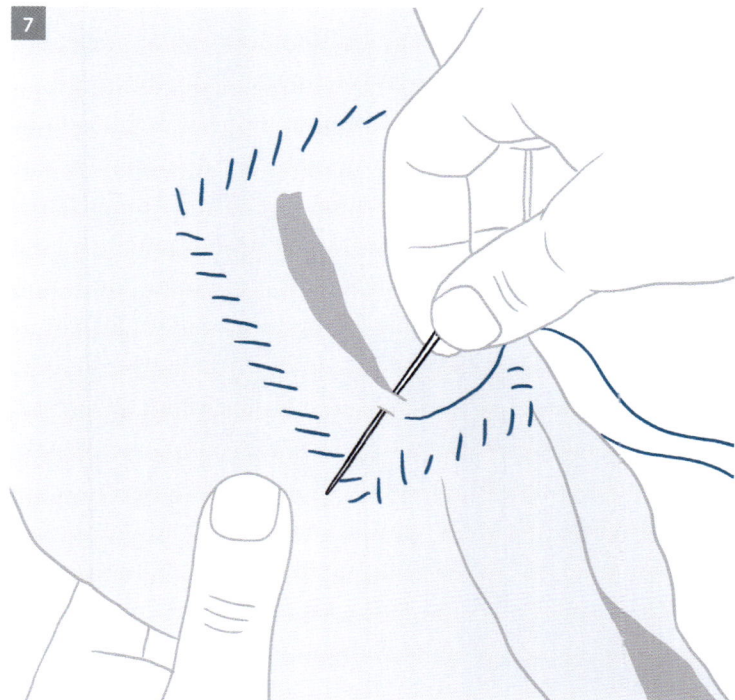

6. Now we can move on to securing the edge of the hole on the right side of the shirt. Turn the sleeve the right way out (RS), thread your needle with a new length of thread and tie a knot in one end. With the hole edges folded under (either basted in place, or tucked in as you work around the hole) you can hide the knotted end of the thread by bringing the needle up through the shirt fabric around 5mm (¼in) away from the folded edge.

7. Push your needle down through the shirt and patch next to the folded edge and angle it to the side to bring it back up again in line with the first stitch. Make sure that you are sewing through both layers of fabric.

8. Continue around the rest of the hole to secure the folded edges and attach the shirt fabric to the patch. When you come back around to the first stitch, make one more evenly spaced stitch before pushing your needle through to the wrong side of your sh rt. Turn the shirt sleeve inside out to trim off the excess thread and knot off.

Collar

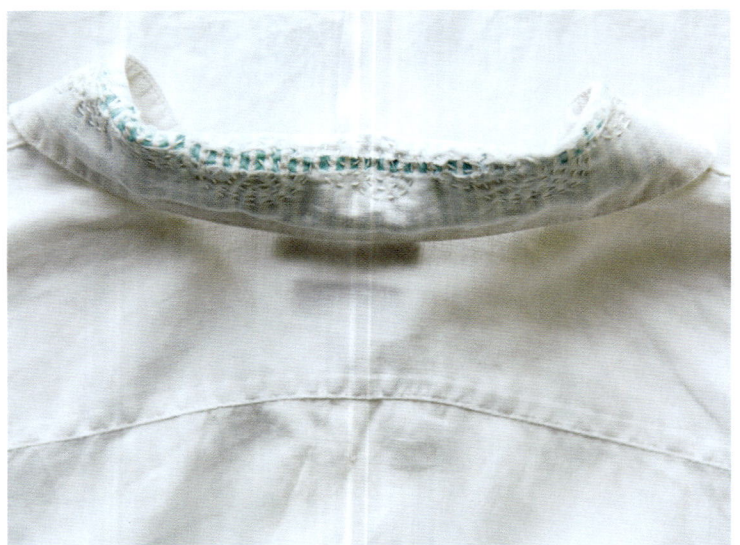

My mend:
A frayed and worn-through collar on a white linen shirt, mended using sashiko and a patch

The wear on a collar often starts very subtly, with colour fading and thinning to the folded edge. As with all clothing repairs, if you can catch it early, adding fabric patches may not be necessary; a simple row of running stitches may be enough to reinforce and strengthen the collar. Another option is to use a seam ripper to unpick the collar from the shirt, flip it over and then stitch it back into place so that the damage is hidden on the underside of the collar when the shirt is worn.

Because the hole covered a large area of this collar, and because collars are made up of two pieces of fabric, I used the hole to my advantage here and sandwiched the fabric patch into the hole between the two layers of fabric. This meant I could make a feature of the damage while strengthening the collar. If the hole is too small to insert the fabric patch, you can simply place the patch on top instead.

The main thing to consider when using a fabric patch on a collar is the weight of the fabric: you'll want to use something relatively thin and soft that will feel comfortable against the back of the neck, and that will not create too much bulk or stiffness, which could alter the way the collar sits.

You will need:
A fabric patch at least 1cm (3/8in) all around bigger than the hole
A sashiko needle
Sashiko cotton or embroidery thread
A fabric marker
Basting thread and hand-sewing needle or pins
An iron

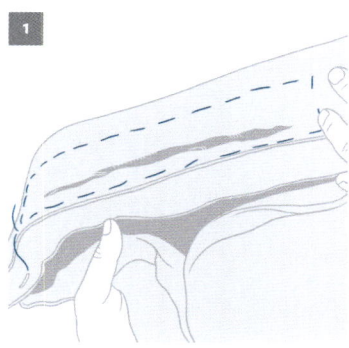 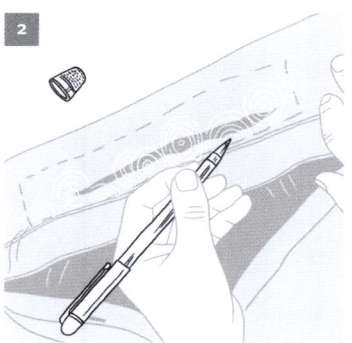

1. Trim any loose threads or particularly frayed edges and then carefully insert the fabric patch in between the collar layers, working gently to ensure the patch lies flat and that you don't cause any further damage to the collar fabric. Once you're happy with the positioning, baste (as shown here) or pin the patch into place.

2. Using a fabric marker, draw out the design you'd like to stitch the patch into place with. I decided to stitch a series of concentric circles here, working organically along the length of the rip. I drew around a thimble for each inner circle and then worked freehand outwards until I was happy with the positioning. You could also use a sashiko template here if you'd prefer to follow a specific pattern.

3. When using sashiko stitches to sew circles or curved designs, you'll need to use a short sashiko needle. Whereas with straight rows of stitching a long needle can be used to pick up several stitches at once, following a curved pattern means it will be more comfortable to use a shorter needle. This will allow you to move more easily around the curves and will create a much smoother finished pattern.

4. Thread your needle and tie a knot in one end. We want to be able to bury this knot in between the fabric patch and collar layers, so put your needle between the layers and push it just through the top layer of shirt fabric near the hole, bringing it up into your starting position on the top of the collar.

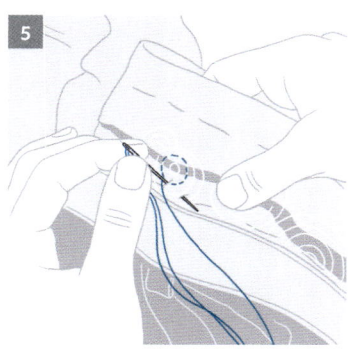
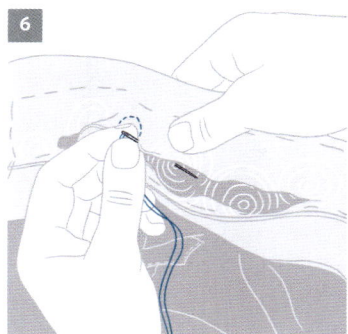
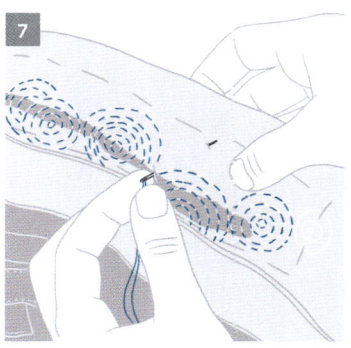

5. With any large rip or tear, you want to ensure that all layers of fabric are lying nice and flat, so it's best to start stitching from the centre of the rip and work outwards. This helps to minimize the chance of the layers of fabric bunching up at one end of the collar. With this pattern, I worked from the centre of the circles outwards, again aiming to keep all layers of fabric flat. Following the fabric marker lines, pick up just one or two stitches at a time to start filling in the circles. If you find that the stitches aren't flowing well enough with the curve of the fabric marker, sew one stitch at a time. When you come back round to your first stitch, insert your needle down into the fabric and then up into position on the marker line on the next circle in the set.

6. Once a full set of circles has been stitched into place, you can use the needle to 'jump' your thread across and into position for the next set. Make sure you don't stitch all the way through, just stitch between the top collar and patch fabric layers.

7. Continue in this way until you have covered all your fabric marker lines. When making your final stitch, insert your needle down and through just the top collar and fabric patch layers, pushing it out and away as far as you can from your final stitch. Pull the needle and thread through, then trim any excess thread. This will bury your thread between the fabric layers without the need to knot the end.

8. Take out the basting stitches and use an iron to remove the fabric marker lines and give the collar a final press.

Underarms

When repairing holes that have materialized close to or along the seams of clothing, I've found it's best to treat each hole as a separate repair rather than lumping them all together. In this instance, on the cross section of a shirt underarm, we have the seam joining the sleeve to itself as well as the seams joining the sleeves and main body: there are three holes that span three different areas of the fabric. Placing one fabric patch across all these holes would restrict the movement that these seams allow when the shirt is worn, and would also feel bulkier.

My mend:
Patches and sashiko stitching to mend the wear and tear on a shirt underarm

You will need:
Fabric patches for each area of damage, at least 1cm (3/8in) bigger than the holes all round
A fine sashiko needle
Sashiko cotton thread or embroidery thread
Basting thread and hand-sewing needle or pins
An iron

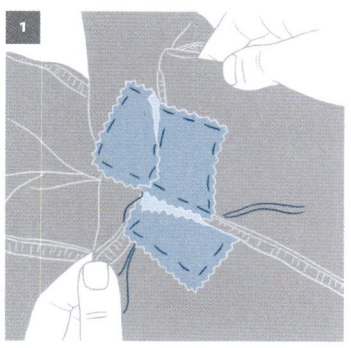
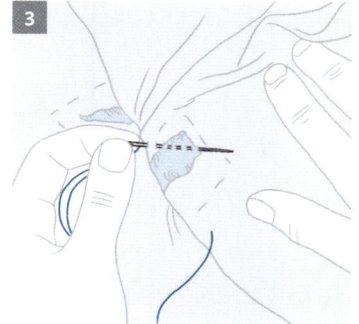
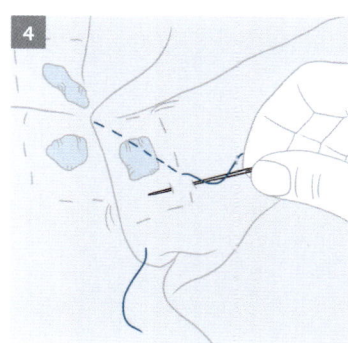
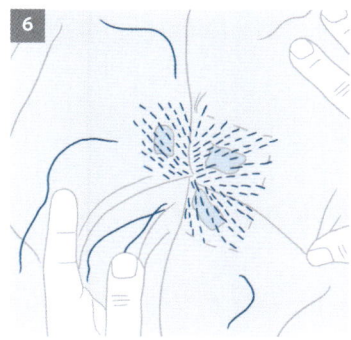
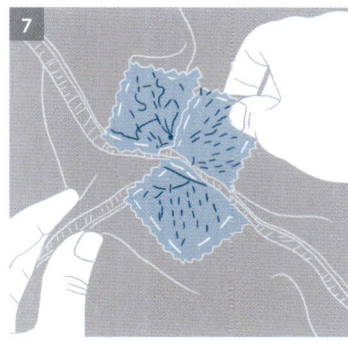

1. To start, trim any loose or frayed edges from the holes, then cut as many fabric patches as needed. Pin or baste them into position on the inside (WS) of the shirt. Raw edges on the patches will work best here to minimize bulk, so use pinking shears for a neater finish.

2. Turn the shirt right side out (RS) and decide whether you want to fold the edges of the holes under (as with the placket repair on page 87) or leave them raw. Thread your needle with your chosen thread.

3. Working one patch at a time, and leaving a tail thread at the side of the patch when you start, begin stitching your chosen stitch design to secure each patch into place.

4. I chose to create a sunburst effect of stitches, so with every section I began stitching from the central crossing point of the seams and worked outwards, to create a fan effect across the wider area. Make sure you sew all the way out to the basting stitches or pins to secure the whole fabric patch into place. Work back and forth in rows until the whole area is covered.

5. Once you have secured the first patch into place, push your needle through to the inside (WS) of the shirt and cut off your thread leaving enough to weave in at the end.

6. Move on to the next patches and repeat the same steps. You can play around with the direction of your stitches across each of the patch repairs here to build up an array of patterns, or choose to have them all running in the same direction.

7. Once all of the patches have been sewn into place and the ends are all woven in, you can remove the basting stitches, trim down any of the patches if needed and weave in all of the tail threads on the inside (WS) of the shirt.

Edges

Wraparound patches are a quick and easy fix if you need to cover up damage on the edges of your clothing. You can fold the edges of your fabric patch under for a clean finish, or leave them raw and let them fray naturally. You can also cut any shape you like! They can be simply sewn into place with a whip stitch along the edges, or secured across the whole patch using sashiko stitches. This repair technique can be used on any edge on a woven item of clothing, from dress hems to shirt cuffs or pocket tops.

The buttonhole stand on this shirt had a hole and tear right at the bottom, so I used a long rectangular piece of fabric to wrap around it; the stand was fairly thinned out so I used a much larger patch than the tear itself. Make sure to use a patch that is lightweight, which won't feel too bulky once sewn on.

You will need:
A fabric patch large enough to wrap around the edge and cover the damage by at least 1cm (⅜in)
A fine sashiko needle
Sashiko cotton thread or embroidery thread
Basting thread and hand-sewing needle or pins

My mend:
A buttonhole stand with a hole and tear, covered with a wraparound patch

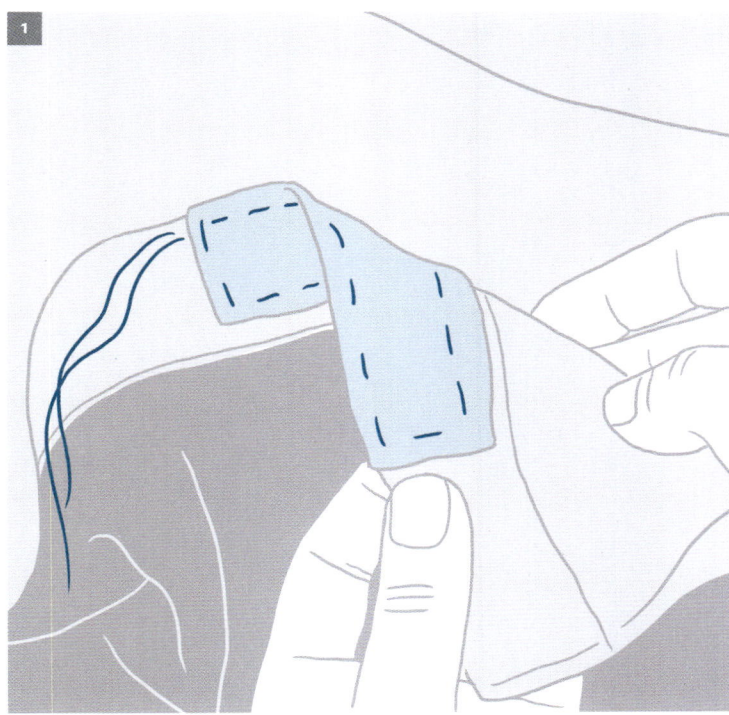
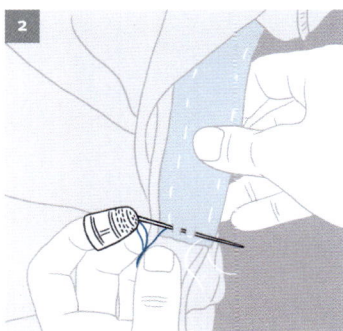
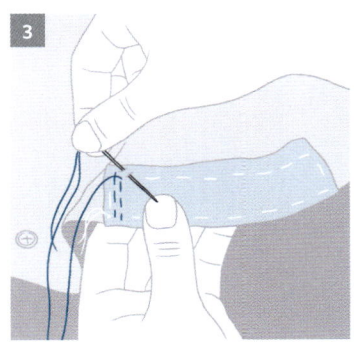

1. To start, cut your fabric patch to size, fold it around the edge of your clothing and baste into place, making sure that the fold of the patch is right up against the edge of the fabric.

2. Thread your needle and tie a knot in one end. On the inside of the shirt (WS), insert your needle through and bring it up into position on the outside (RS) of your shirt in one corner of your fabric patch furthest away from the edge. Sew a line of small running stitches, working from the edge of the patch across to the edge of the shirt and folded patch edge, making sure to sew through all layers of the fabric patch and shirt fabric.

3. As you make the final stitch on this row, angle your needle so that you can bring it through and up into position ready to start your next row.

4. Repeat this process to cover the whole fabric patch, checking as you work that you are stitching through all layers, and that the edge isn't being stretched or distorted out of shape. When you reach the end of the patch, push your needle through to the inside of the shirt and weave the thread into a few of the stitches on the inside, then trim off the excess thread.

4 *T-shirts*

T-shirts don't generally find themselves with too much obvious wear and tear; they've been designed to be simple, hard-wearing garments and, depending on the quality of the jersey, can last damage free for several years. However, they are prone to moth holes and tiny nicks, as well as an all-too-common hole and laddering issue around the bottom centre. The cause? The jeans zipper! People always seem surprised by this, but I've lost count of how many T-shirts have ended up at workshops with me with very similar holes all in the same location.

Patches

My mend:
Moth holes in a T-shirt body, mended with patches and open backstitch

Although they're small to start with, moth holes can quickly stretch and ruin a perfectly good T-shirt. If the hole is too small to darn, then a small patch is a great alternative. You will need small fabric scraps of a similar weight and stretch to the T-shirt you are repairing. If the holes are really close together you could use one larger patch and baste this into place around all holes. These will be sewn into place using an open backstitch – similar to the seed stitch used for reinforcing leggings (see page 114). This is a simple stitch that adds strength, but still allows stretch and movement, so it's perfect for stretchy fabrics.

You will need:

A fabric patch (or patches) of a similar weight and stretch to the T-shirt
A ball-tipped needle or a very fine sashiko needle
Fine sashiko cotton thread or embroidery thread
Basting thread and hand-sewing needle or pins

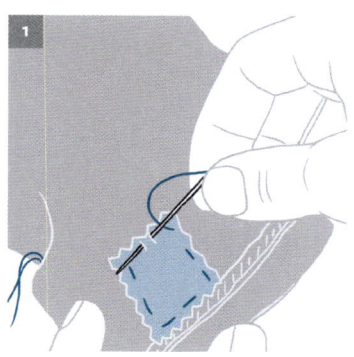 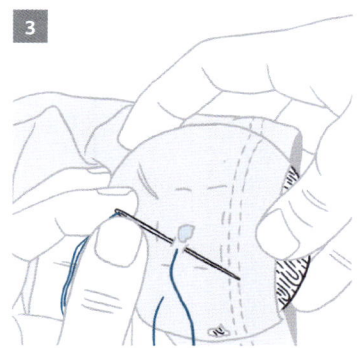 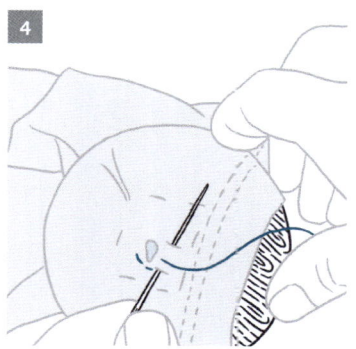

1. Trim the fabric scrap so that it is larger than the hole by about 1cm (³⁄₈in) all around, and baste it into place on the inside (WS) of the T-shirt with the patch RS down. If the hole and patch are small enough, you may find this step unnecessary and can just go straight into stitching the patch, holding it in position as you sew.

2. With the T-shirt turned right side out, bring your needle up from the inside of the T-shirt to the outside near the edge of the patch, ensuring you have caught both the T-shirt fabric and the fabric scrap. Leave a tail of thread on the RS to be woven in at the end.

3. With these smaller moth holes and repairs, aim for your stitch length to be around 2–3mm (¹⁄₁₂in), so that the proportions of the stitches match the hole size. To create your first stitch, push the needle down through the fabric a stitch length *behind* where you have pulled the needle through, rather than in front of it. Bring your needle back up on the other side of this stitch, leaving a gap that will allow for the next stitch as well as the gap between the stitches – so the gap should be a double stitch length.

4. Continue to sew small stitches in this way, one at a time, around the moth hole on the outside of the shirt, securing the fabric patch into place. You could do one circle of stitches or build up a few circles to add extra detail.

5. As you make your last stitch, push your needle out to the edge of the repair. You can now turn your T-shirt inside out (WS), then pull the tail threads through to weave them in (see page 35). If you are mending more than one hole, repeat the steps for the next hole.

NOTE: With standard backstitch, the aim is a solid line of evenly sized stitches, but with open backstitch, we want the finished stitches to look like a running stitch with a gap between each stitch. For a standard backstitch, you create your stitches by working back to front; this creates a loop effect to the stitches on the wrong side of the fabric, as opposed to a running stitch, which is just a linear line of thread. Working the backstitch this way creates a stronger repair that also maintains the element of stretch we need.

Shaped darns

My mend:
Wear and tear to a T-shirt sleeve, covered over using a shaped darn

Once you are comfortable with the foundations of a standard darn, you can start experimenting with all sorts of shaped darns – circles, hearts, triangles, the choice is yours! These are so much fun to play around with, especially when working to cover several moth holes on a T-shirt, as you can create really graphic darns to complement the garment. Try using a range of different colours similar to the patchwork of darns shown on the green cardigan in Chapter 2 (see page 72), or stick to one colour as I have done here to embellish the T-shirt in a simple way with a pop of colour.

You will need:
A fine darning needle or a ball-tipped needle
Embroidery thread (split into fewer strands if necessary to match the weight of the T-shirt)
A darning mushroom or disc and an elastic tie
A fabric marker

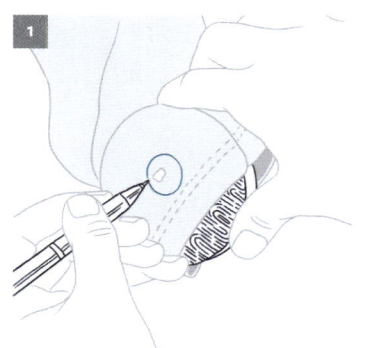
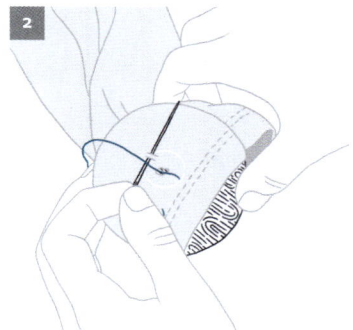
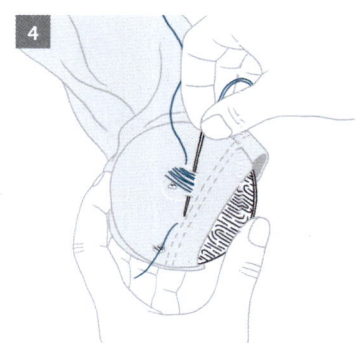

1. With the T-shirt right side out, insert the darning mushroom or disc under the hole and secure it with an elastic tie, if using. Make sure that the fabric tension feels nice and even, and is not pulled too tightly. Using a fabric marker, start by marking out the area you are planning to darn. You can work freehand if you're creating a darn that organically follows the shape of the hole, but guidelines can help when creating a shaped darn.

NOTE: In this example I'm darning a circular area, so I'm starting the warp threads in the centre of the circle. This will help to create an even darn, which is great if you're making a shape that needs to be symmetrical, and starting in the middle with your weft rows too will also help create a smoother finished shape.

2. Bring your needle up from the edge of the darning mushroom and into position at the bottom centre of the shape and pull it through, remembering to leave a tail of thread to be woven in later. You'll stitch your vertical warp threads using the shape you have drawn as your guide. Take your needle down at the top of the circle and back up again at a thread's width distance on the circle line to set your needle back up for the next row. This will create a tiny stitch on the reverse of the fabric.

3. Now bring the needle back down in line with your first stitch to create the second warp row. Continue in this way, following the shape you have marked out, making sure that the gaps between your warp stitches are even – they should be about the width of your thread. If you are darning a finer stretch fabric, make sure that your needle isn't pulling or stretching the fabric out too much as you sew. As always, check on the overall tension every few rows.

4. Once you have finished one half of the circle, go back to the centre and repeat this process to fill in the other side. To keep your circle even, take note of the number of warp threads on the half you have already done, and try to mirror this for the second half.

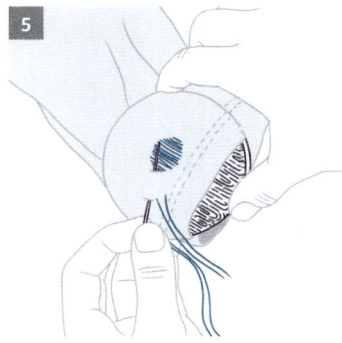

5. Repeat until you reach the end of the circle, then pull the thread through and out to the side of your fabric. You are now ready to start weaving in the weft threads. Bring your needle up through the fabric next to and in the middle of the warp thread on one side.

SHAPED DARNS 103

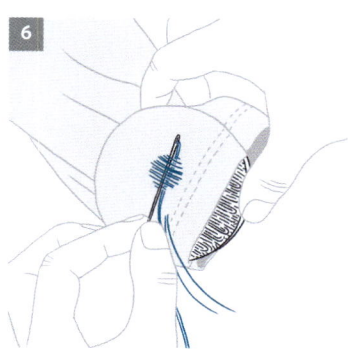
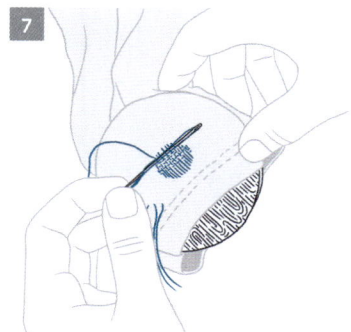
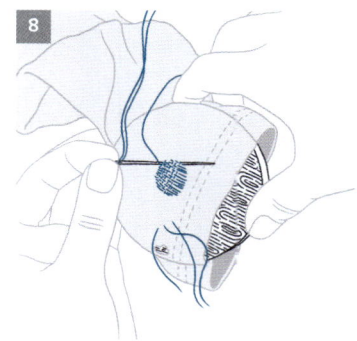

6. If using a sharp-pointed needle, turn the needle around to weave with the eye of the needle and start weaving over and under your warp threads until you reach the other side of the circle. Push your needle down through the fabric to secure this row into place and up again just above this, ready to go back and weave the second row. Remember to alternate the order in which you weave over and under each warp thread. If you went over the warp thread on the first row, for this row you will go under it, and vice versa.

7. Continue in this way working up the top half of the circle; as you do this, each weft row will become shorter as you have fewer warp threads to weave in and out of. Use the drawn outline of your shape at the end of each weft row as a guide to where to insert the needle to secure your darn into place.

8. When you reach the top of the circle, insert your needle to secure the final weft row, then bring it back up into position, ready to fill in the bottom half of the circle.

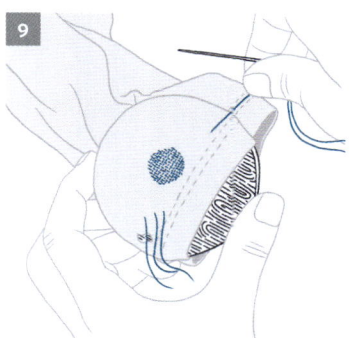

9. When you have filled in the rest of the warp threads, bring your needle down and out at the edge of your darning mushroom to finish the front of your darn.

10. Remove your fabric from the darning mushroom and turn it inside out (WS). Use your needle to pull the tail threads through to the inside and weave them in (see page 35).

SHAPED DARNS 105

Necklines

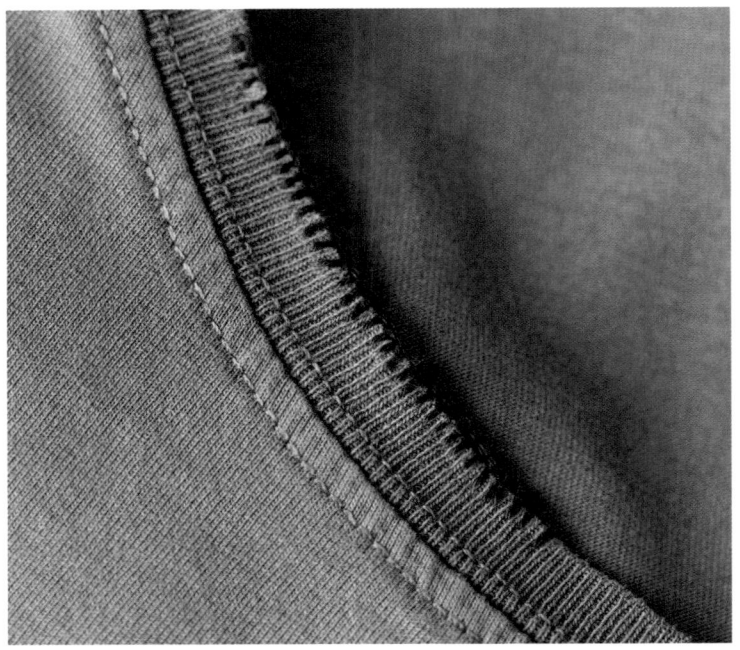

My mend:
A frayed T-shirt neckline

You will need:
A ball-tipped needle or fine sashiko needle
Sashiko cotton or embroidery thread

On thin T-shirts the necklines can wear out pretty quickly, leaving small fine holes along the edge of the fabric. When these holes cover a large section of the neckline, the best option is to remove it and replace the entire neck with a new piece of ribbing, but if this isn't an option I've spent some time experimenting with some hand-sewn options that work as well.

Patching over small areas can be a good option, and wrapping a piece of fabric over the edge of the neckline to secure the edge in place will stop the holes from getting any worse (as shown on page 96). However, the fabric patch you use will need to be very lightweight so as not to be uncomfortable against the neck, and maintaining the natural stretch of the neckline is also really important.

Blanket stitch is the easiest and most effective option, as you can make super-small stitches that are close enough together to cover the holes well and help the stitches blend into the rib of the neckline. (You can also use this technique on worn hemlines.)

You can use basic blanket stitch or crossed blanket stitch, which adds extra detail. Depending on the condition of the neckline, I'd recommend trying both options and seeing how the stitches lie against the neckline: you want to choose the stitch that causes the least amount of distortion. Both are described here.

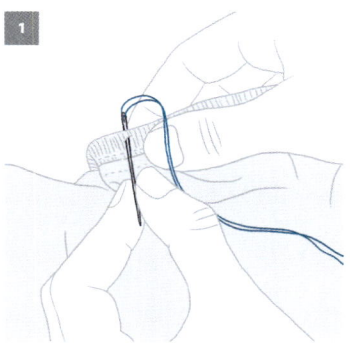 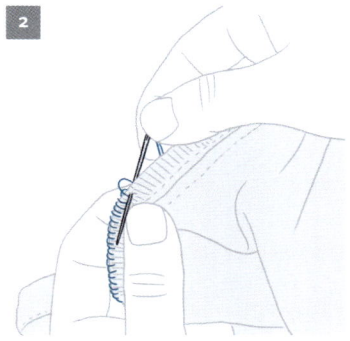 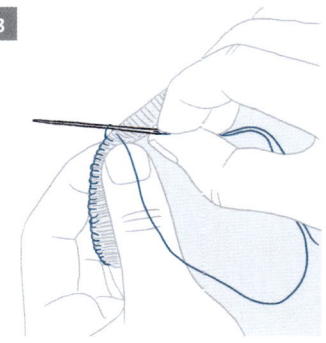

1. Thread your needle and tie a knot at the end, then bring your needle through from the inside of the fabric edge (WS) to the outside (RS), around 3–5mm (⅛–¼in) away from the edge.

NOTE: Whether you are sewing left to right or right to left across the neckline will determine which way you insert the needle through the loop to create the blanket stitch. As I am left-handed, I work from left to right, which means that I insert the needle through the loop from right to left. If you are right-handed, insert the needle through the loop from left to right.

2. For basic blanket stitch, from the inside of the fabric, push your needle through and out again in the same place as your first stitch. This time, when you pull the thread through, leave a small loop of thread instead of pulling all the way through. Put your needle through this loop and then pull through. Move along the fabric edge – around 3mm (⅛in) is a good width for the gap between each stitch, as you want the frayed edges to be as covered as possible – and bring your needle through again from the inside of the fabric through to the front.

3. When you have a small loop left as you pull the thread through, insert your needle through the loop, then pull through to secure the stitch as before. Repeat these steps across the length of the fabric edge until you reach the end of the damaged area.

4. Make one last stitch so that the needle and thread end up on the inside of the neckline. To do this, bring your needle through from the inside to the outside, once again pushing your needle through the loop of thread to make one last blanket stitch. Then push your needle down from the outside to the inside over that last stitch, bringing your needle to the inside edge. Tie a knot in the thread here and then trim off the excess.

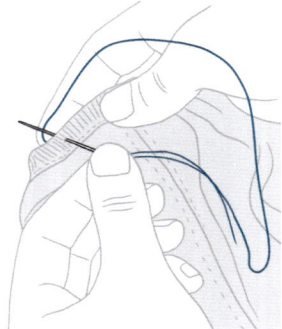

5. For a little more detail, you could use a crossed blanket stitch instead. With your needle threaded, insert it from the side of where you want your stitches to start between the layers of the neckline (so that the tail thread is buried between these layers) and up through to the top of the folded edge of the neckline.

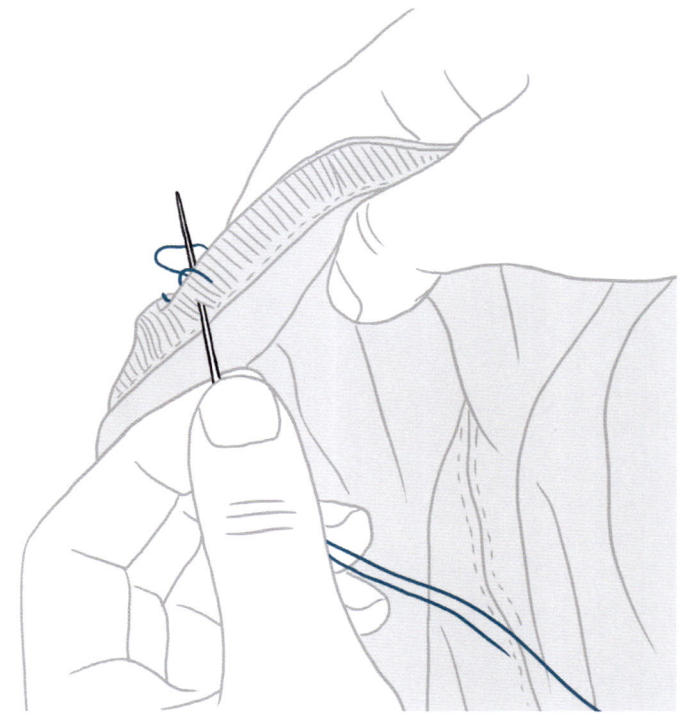

6. Decide on the size you want for these stitches. I chose 5mm (¼in) to be in proportion with the rib of the neckline. Make a stitch diagonally down and then back up again, bringing your needle out right next to where you started at the top folded edge of the neckline. As you pull your needle and thread through, make sure that your thread is underneath the needle so that you loop through and catch it, as with a standard blanket stitch.

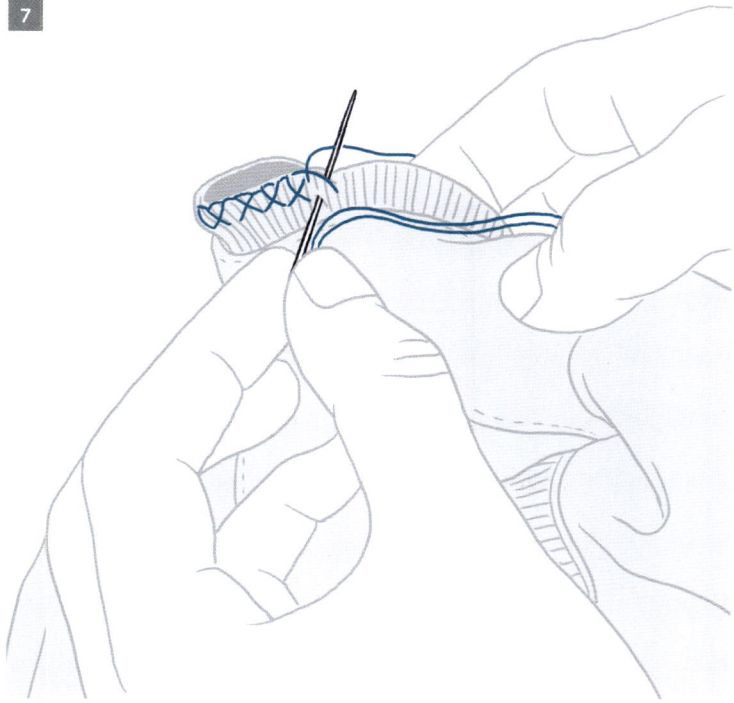

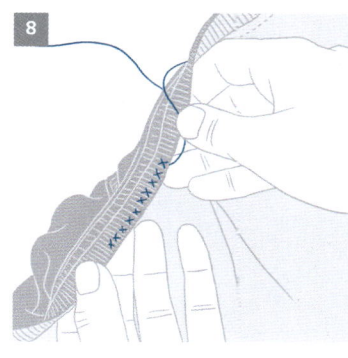

8. When you reach the end of the damaged area, make one final cross stitch and then bring your needle down and through to the inside (WS) of the T-shirt to weave in the ends (see page 35). The inside (WS) of your fabric will show a small row of crosses.

7. You'll now make a second stitch to cross the first one. Line your needle up with the bottom of the first stitch and bring your needle down through the fabric, then up again at the folded edge of the fabric, again in line with the first diagonal stitch. Pull your needle and thread through again, remembering to catch the thread as before. These two steps make up one cross stitch and are repeated across the edge of the fabric.

Remember to pull the threads through slowly with each stitch so that you don't distort the natural shape of the neckline, and check that the crossed blanket stitches that build up along the edge of the fabric are evenly spaced.

5 *Leggings*

Leggings have been one of the most requested items of clothing to share repair techniques for in the last few years. They're a staple in most wardrobes, but tend to wear thin very quickly at the thighs and at the knees, and the extra stretchy cotton-Lycra mix can be tricky to mend. As with T-shirts and socks, maintaining stretch is the key factor to remember when repairing them. Every repair needs to work with the stretch and not restrict it to ensure a long-lasting fix, and it's also important not to use bulky patches that will be uncomfortable when worn against the skin.

Crotch & thighs

You will need:
A stretchy fabric patch big enough to allow a 1-cm (⅜-in) margin all round the hole
A fine cotton darning needle, a fine sharp needle or a ball-tipped needle
Embroidery thread split into fewer strands, or fine sashiko thread
A darning mushroom or tailor's ham and tie
Fabric marker (optional)

My mend:
Leggings that have worn thin at the thigh, repaired using patches and seed stitch

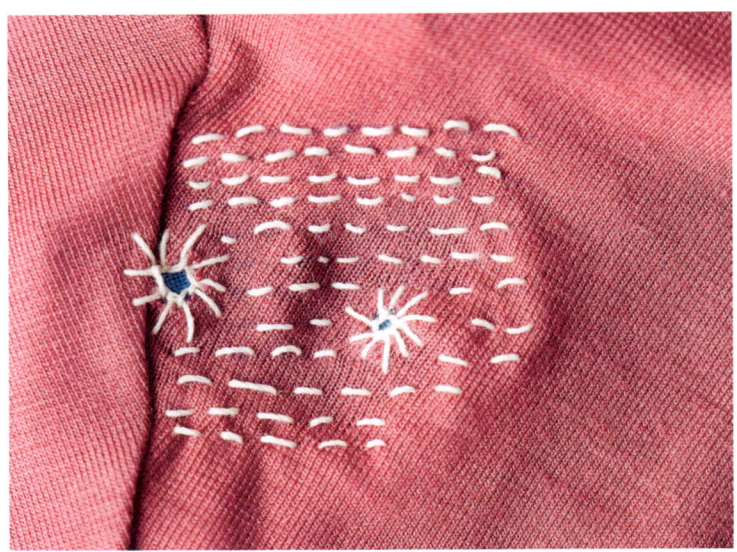

If you're looking to repair a pair of leggings in which large holes have already formed at the crotch seams, you can use the patching techniques shown in Chapter 1. Remember that you'll need to use fabric patches that are of a similar weight and stretch to the garment. I'd also recommend reinforcing any seams on a sewing machine or with a simple running stitch.

An alternative, seed stitch, which is worked in the same way as the open backstitch shown on page 101, is a super-simple hand sewing stitch to use on stretchy fabrics that have worn thin. It's a secure stitch that maintains the element of stretch that is so important in creating a long-lasting repair. To create a discreet but strong repair to the thighs of leggings, you can work seed stitch in a series of parallel rows in line with the stretch of the leggings, or stitch organically in any direction for a confetti-like finish.

The leggings in this repair had worn thin all around the two small holes, so I decided to combine two techniques for a stronger finish. The small flower-like repairs were worked first using a blanket stitch with a patch underneath to reinforce the holes, and seed stitch was worked afterwards to strengthen the surrounding weakened fabric.

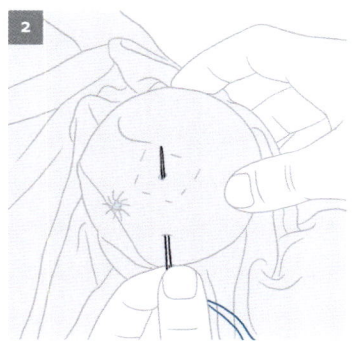 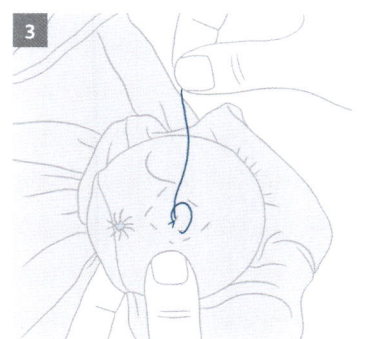 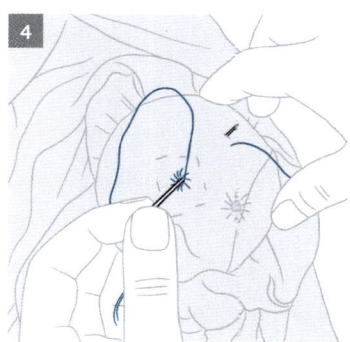

1. With the leggings inside out (WS), baste a small fabric patch into place underneath the hole. I find that basting works much better than pinning with stretchy fabrics, but be careful not to stretch the fabric out of shape as you do this, and use a thin needle to avoid damaging the fabric. Now turn right side out (RS). Use a darning mushroom or a tailor's ham underneath the leggings with an elastic tie to hold it into place. Make sure not to overstretch the fabric here – you want it to lie fairly naturally, and not be pulled out of shape.

2. With your needle threaded, bring it through from the side of the leggings into position through the patch fabric and in line with the edge of the hole where you want to start stitching. Leave a tail of thread to be woven in later.

3. Work blanket stitch around the edge of the hole by bringing your needle down through the leggings fabric, then up into position next to the first stitch on the patch fabric, in line with the edge of the hole. As you pull the stitch through, make sure that the thread is underneath your needle so that it catches and creates the blanket stitch. (I am working in a counterclockwise direction.)

4. Continue to work around the hole, checking the tension of your fabric and stitches. When you come back to the first stitch, push your needle through and out to the side of your darning disc.

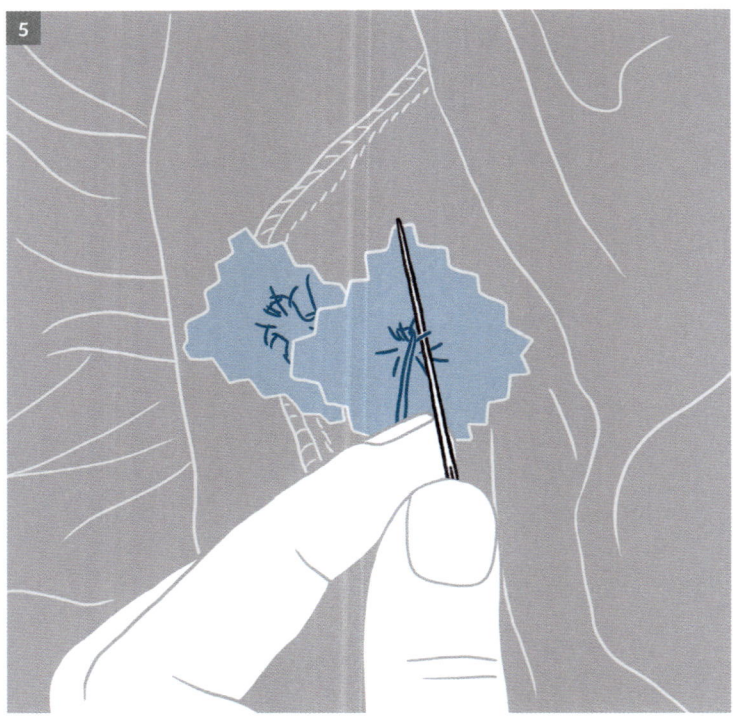

5. Remove the disc and band and turn your leggings inside out again to weave in the tail threads.

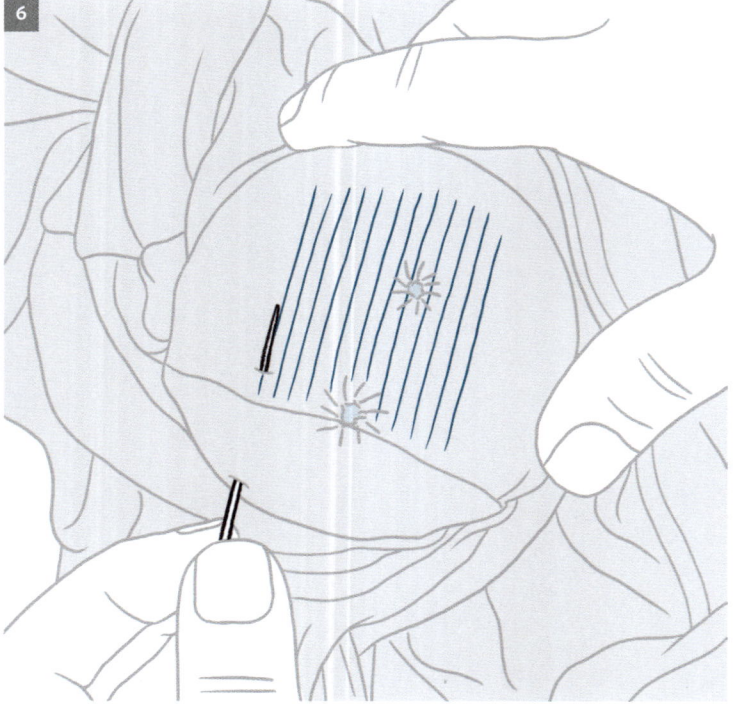

6. Turn right side out again and reposition the darning disc and band ready to start working the seed stitch. I chose to work a series of lines around the holes and marked them out with a fabric pen, but, as previously mentioned, you can work these stitches in any direction for a random patterned finish.

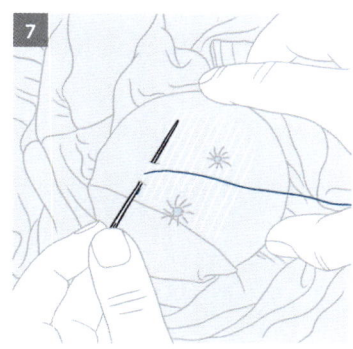

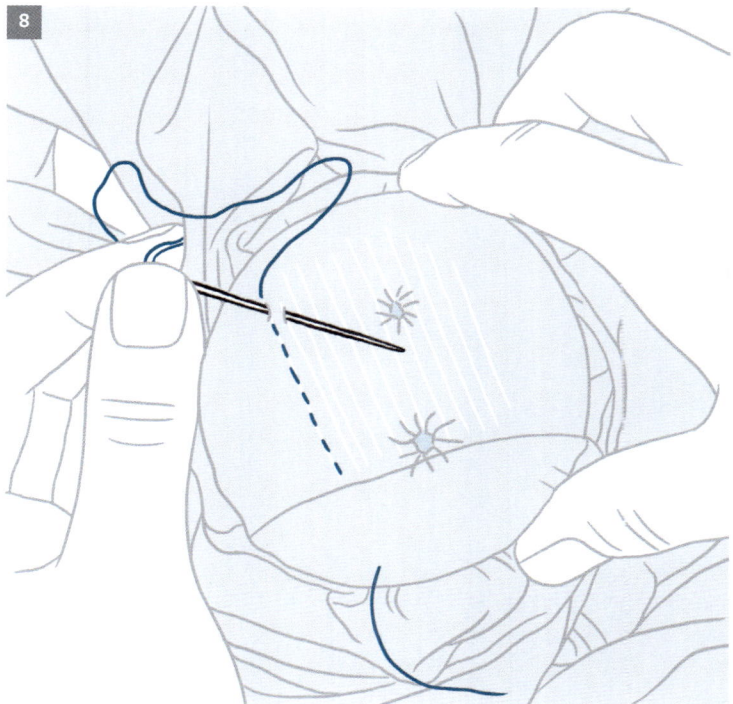

7. As with backstitch, create your first stitch by pushing your needle down and through the fabric *behind* your thread rather than in front of it. Bring the needle back up into position where you want the second stitch to start. Continue in this way, building up a series of stretchy seed stitches all across the weakened fabric, following the marked lines or stitching randomly.

8. When you reach the end of the first row, bring your needle up a stitch length along the second row, to allow you to continue backstitching along the row.

NOTE: Make sure that you don't jump too far across the fabric between each stitch: around 5mm – 1cm (¼–⅜in) is ideal to create that nice stretchy finish without creating big loops on the inside of the leggings.

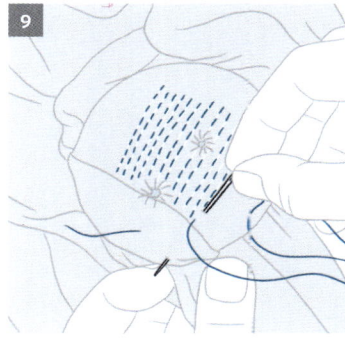

9. When you have covered the whole area, push your needle down through the fabric and out to the side to finish.

10. Remove the darning mushroom and tie and turn the leggings inside out (WS) to pull the tail threads through and weave them in (see page 35).

Main body

When I'm shown damaged leggings, small annoying snags and tears seem to be the most common fault after wearing thin at the crotch and thigh area. These holes can be easy to ignore when small, but they can quickly stretch, requiring a more involved repair, so where possible try to fix them at this stage.

(If you need to cover a larger hole in leggings, you can use the patching techniques covered in Chapters 1 and 3. You'll need to match the stretch of the leggings with the patches, and make sure not to restrict the stretch of the leggings once the patch is in place.)

I love the look and texture of chain stitch and I think it works brilliantly as a surface repair to cover these small holes, while allowing you to have fun with the colours and shapes of the stitches. It's a great stitch to use on stretchy fabrics as it won't restrict the stretch too much. Sports leggings patterns are often bold and graphic, so you can use that as a starting point to create a repair that complements the design.

My mend:
Holes in a pair of leggings, mended using chain stitch

You will need:
A short, fine darning needle or a fine sharps needle
Embroidery thread split down to 1 strand
A darning disc or a tailor's ham
Fabric marker pen (optional)

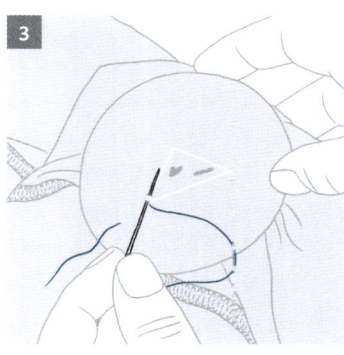

3. To make your first stitch, push your needle back down right next to where you brought the needle and thread up, then bring it back up again along your marked line. Aim for the stitches to be around 2–3mm (1/12–1/8in) long.

1. Insert a darning disc or tailor's ham on the inside (WS) of the leggings and secure in place with a hairband or an elastic tie. Make sure you don't stretch the fabric too tightly; you want it to lie nice and flat so that the repair doesn't distort it. If you want to create a particular shape, I recommend drawing it onto the fabric with a fabric marker so that you have an easy guide to follow.

2. Thread your needle and insert it from the side of the darning disc through to the right side (RS) of the fabric into position where you want to start stitching, remembering to leave a tail of thread to be woven in later.

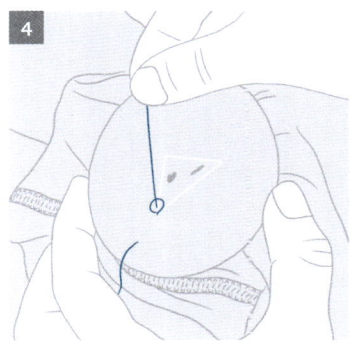

4. As you pull the thread through for this first stitch, position the thread underneath your needle so that as you pull the needle through you catch a small loop of thread. This is your first chain stitch.

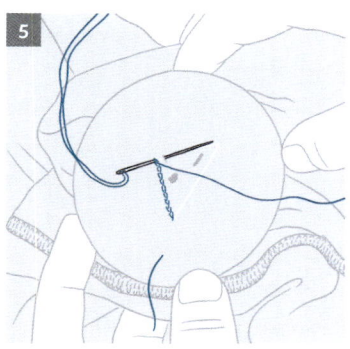 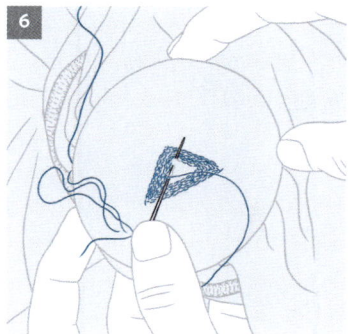 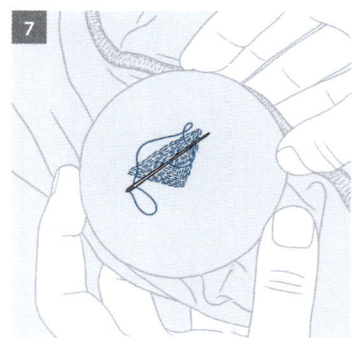

5. Push your needle back down into this loop again as close as possible to the previous stitch, then back up again, moving further along your marked line and, again, catching the loop of thread. Repeat these steps until you reach the first corner or edge of your shape (if you're making a circle, you can just continue to spiral the stitches inwards until you reach the centre). Make one last stitch on the line you're on, and then angle your needle down and back up again to start working along the next line.

6. Continue in this way, working inwards to fill the whole area. As you approach the hole or snag in the fabric, make the stitches as close as you can to the edge of the fabric and then skip over the hole until you can make your next stitch into fabric on the other side.

7. When you reach the centre of your shape, make one last stitch, then secure that final stitch by pushing your needle down on the outside of the chain and out to the side of the fabric.

NOTE: As these sports leggings have a 4-way stretch, every time I inserted the needle the fabric wanted to move and be pulled around. Be sure to check the tension every few stitches to make sure that the fabric isn't being pulled too tightly or is puckering as you stitch.

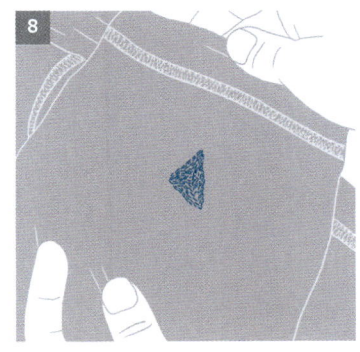

8. Remove the darning disc or tailor's ham, turn the leggings inside out and pull the tail threads through to the inside ready to weave in (see page 35) and trim.

MAIN BODY

6 *Socks*

Socks tend to wear out in similar places for most of us: the back of the heel, the soles of the feet and at the toes. Most socks contain elastane, regardless of whether they're cotton, wool, bamboo or synthetic, as it's that elastic stretch that helps ensure a comfy fit. This means that when it comes to repairing damaged socks you'll need to remember to allow for the stretch – it's better to have a slightly looser weave than one that is too tight and puckers and pulls at the rest of the sock. Honeycomb darning is also a great technique for sock repairs, particularly if you use it to reinforce thinned-out areas that have not yet turned into a hole; it will add strength and can be worked in large areas fairly quickly.

Heels

Darning from the front is one of my favourite techniques, as there are so many ways you can get creative and make it your own. In this example, I have made small running stitches all around the patch, before each warp and weft thread; you can omit these, however, as shown in shaped darns on page 102.

These small design choices are what make visible mending such an interesting form of textile art: every decision we make when mending will be influenced by the area of damage we are fixing. You can go further by adding several lines of extra stitches all around your patch to add extra reinforcement to thinned-out areas of fabric. You can stitch organically or follow the knit stitches (take a look at the green cardigan in Chapter 2, page 70, for examples of this). These extra stitches help to create a really embedded darn once finished.

My mend:
A plain-weave darn applied to a worn-out sock heel

You will need:
Yarn or thread of a similar weight and matching fibre content to the sock
A cotton or tapestry darning needle to match the weight of the yarn
A darning mushroom or disc

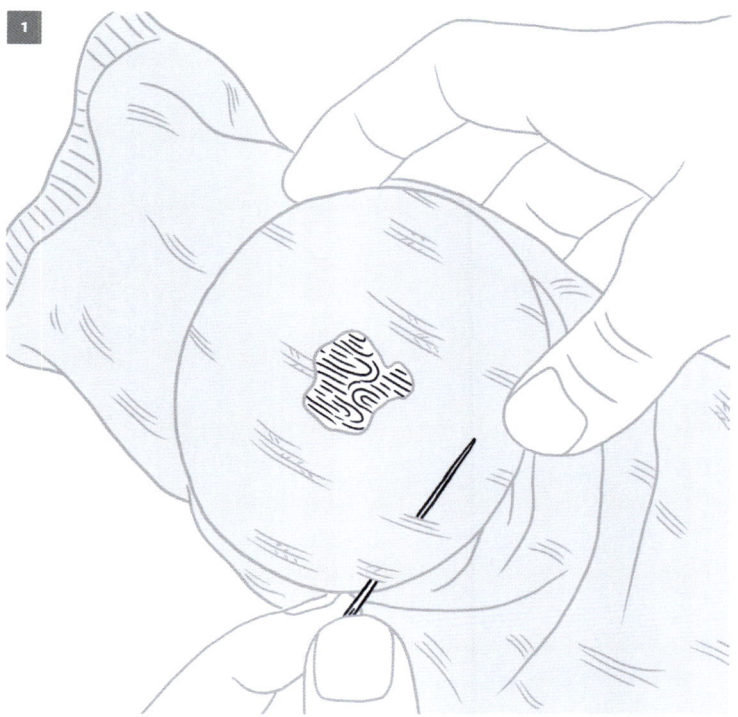

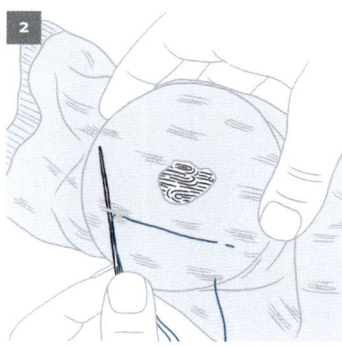

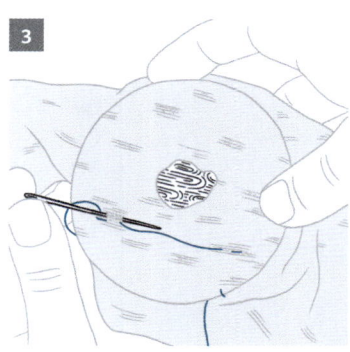

1. Insert a darning mushroom or disc underneath the hole and secure into place with an elastic tie if using. Make sure that the fabric tension feels nice and even, and is not pulled too tightly. Bring your needle down near the edge of the darning mushroom and back up in the area of the mend, making a small vertical stitch just below the area you want your darn to start, leaving a tail of thread to be woven in later. Remember to allow extra space around the area of damage for these running stitches, as you still want the warp and weft threads to be at least 1cm (3⁄8in) away from the damage.

2. Work out how long you need your warp threads to be, stitch your first long warp thread, then secure it by going back under your fabric and creating another small stitch in line with it, as you did at the start.

3. Push your needle down and up at the side (this will make a tiny stitch on the inside of the sock), into position to create your second warp thread, starting with a small running stitch again. The gap between each row should be around the width of your thread to ensure an evenly filled darn.

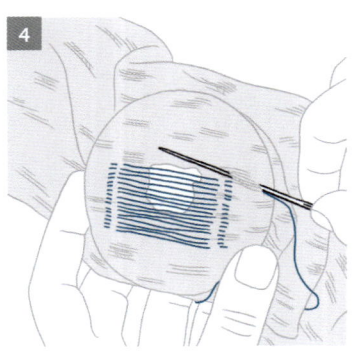 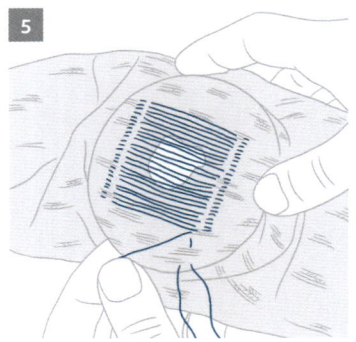 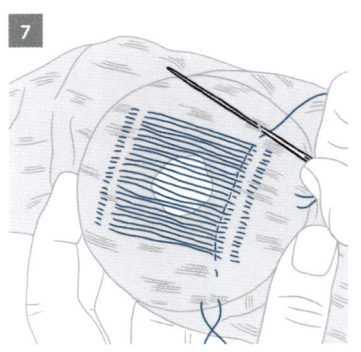

4. Continue in this way until you have covered the area to darn with long warp threads secured with running stitches at their ends. If you run out of thread or want to add a new thread colour, simply bring your needle down and out at the edge of your darning mushroom as you did at the start, and then bring it with the new colour, leaving a tail thread in the same way.

5. To start your horizontal weft rows, use a new piece of thread and bring your needle up from the edge of the darning mushroom, creating a small running stitch as before. Bring your needle back up and into position to start weaving in one of the bottom corners, right next to the first warp thread that you made.

6. If your needle is sharp, turn it around so that you are using the eye of the needle. Weave over and under the warp threads alternately: over one, under one, over one, under one, and so on. (Using the eye of the needle helps make sure that you don't catch or snag any of the warp threads or fibres underneath as you are weaving).

7. When you reach the end of the warp threads, secure the weft thread down at the edge of your warp threads by pushing your needle through the fabric and up again (as you did when creating the warp rows) ready to create your small running stitch to the side. You can then move your needle down through the fabric and up into position above this stitch ready to start the next row.

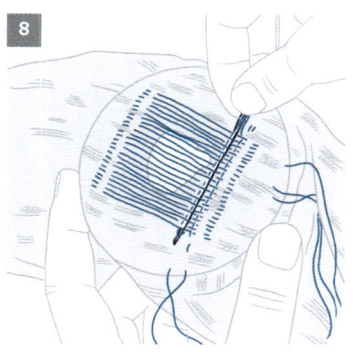 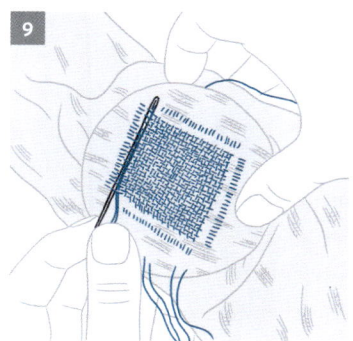 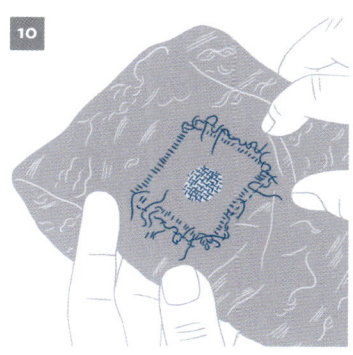

8. Create a small running stitch, then go back across your warp threads, this time alternating the order in which you go over and under the threads. Repeat these steps until you have filled all your warp threads. As you build up the weft rows, once you have woven your needle through all of the warp threads but before you pull it through, use the length of your needle to push down the threads of the previous row. This will help to create a really even weave.

9. As you get closer to the top of the warp threads it will become harder to weave through them, but try to push your weft threads down so that the darn is tight and filled in. Continue until you can no longer weave the needle under and over your warp threads.

10. When you reach the end of your darn, bring your needle down through the fabric at the corner next to the last warp thread, create a final running stitch, and then bring it out at the edge of your darning mushroom. Remove your fabric from the darning mushroom and turn it inside out (WS) in order to weave in the tail threads.

Toes

You will need:
Yarn or embroidery thread of a similar weight and matching fibre content to the sock
A darning needle to match the weight of the yarn
A darning mushroom or disc
Fabric marker (optional)

My mend:
Wear and tear to sock toes, repaired using honeycomb darning

Honeycomb darning looks great from both sides, and also lies flat to the surface of the garment, making it a comfortable option for mending items of clothing that are worn close to the skin. It uses blanket stitches worked in circular rounds on top of the fabric instead of at the edge or hem, and is a good way to reinforce threadbare fabrics before a hole has worn through.

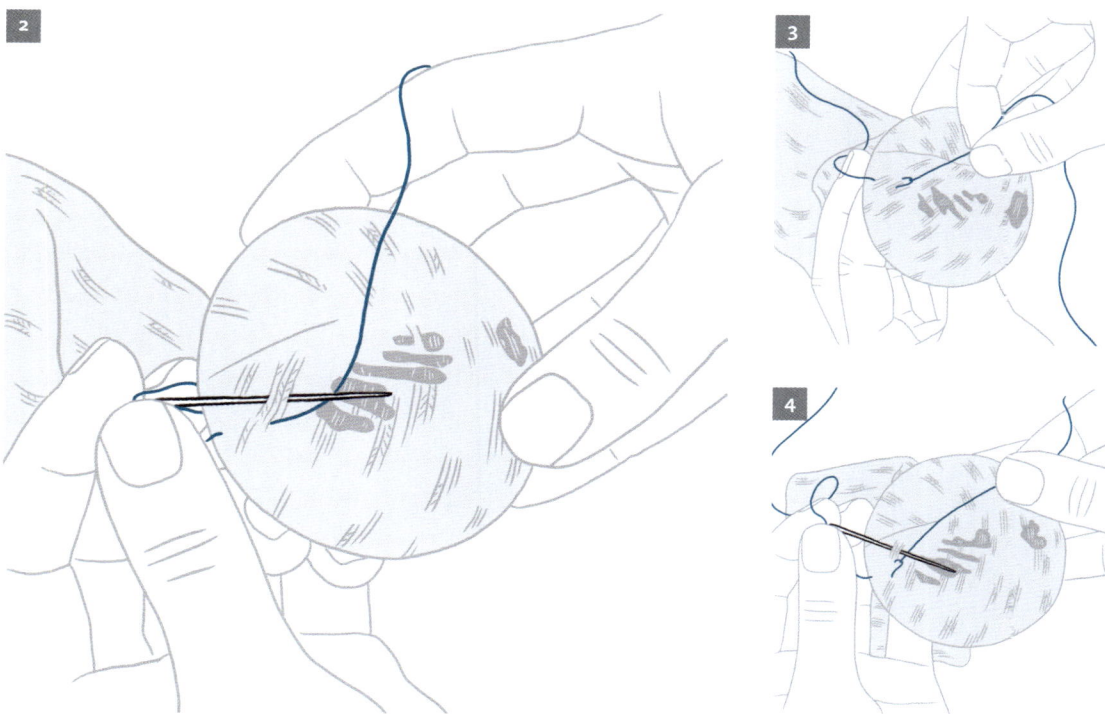

1. Prepare your sock by inserting the darning mushroom or disc underneath the hole and securing it into place with an elastic tie, if needed. Make sure that the fabric tension feels nice and even and is not pulled too tight. You can either follow the shape of the area you are repairing freehand, as I have, or mark out a shape with a fabric marker as a guide to follow.

2. Bring your needle up from the edge of your darning mushroom and into position at least 1cm (⅜in) away from the area of damage. Make a small stitch about 5mm (¼in) to the side of where your thread is by pushing your needle down and up again, angling the needle down towards the hole.

3. As you pull the needle through, make sure that your thread is underneath the needle as shown above – this will catch your stitch, creating a loop that you will secure into place with your next stitch. The first stitch will be secured into place when starting the second round of stitches, so don't worry about this for now.

4. Repeat this step, making your next stitch alongside this one and remembering to pull your needle through with the thread underneath it, creating a loop and securing it into place.

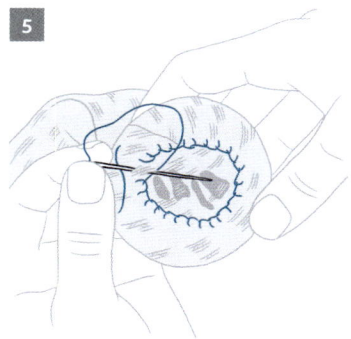

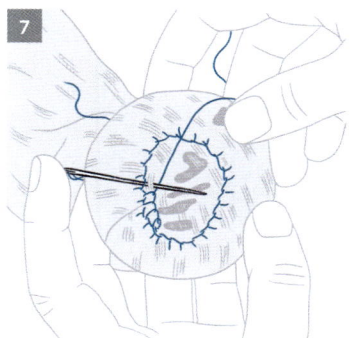

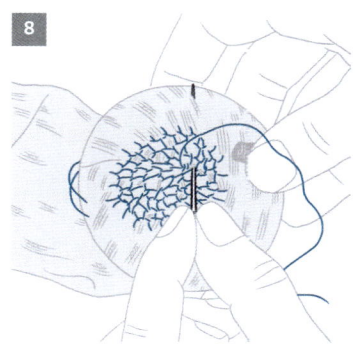

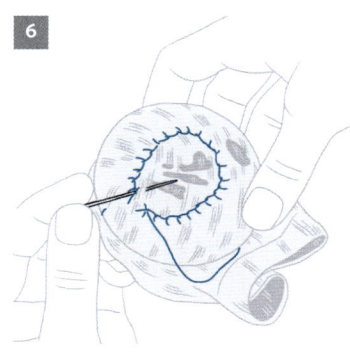

5. Continue in this way around the shape you are working towards until you end up back at the beginning.

6. When you make your last stitch on this first round, bring your needle down to mark the start of the next round of stitches, at the same time as catching the first stitch you made to secure it into place.

7. The next round of stitches are worked in the same way, but this time you have the previous round as a guide instead of your marked line. Aim to make each downward stitch for this round in the middle of the horizontal stitches from the first round, as shown.

NOTE: If you are repairing thinned-out fabric, continue in this way all the way to the centre, making sure to push your needle through the fabric as you work. If you are covering a hole, you will reach a point where there is no fabric for you to sew into. In this instance, you simply need to work into the previous round of stitches created, making sure not to pull any threads too tightly and alter the tension. Working honeycomb darning this way creates a really densely filled patch compared to stitching directly through the fabric, which gives you more flexibility to create a slightly looser patch.

8. Continue in this way until you have filled your shape and reached the centre. To finish, insert your needle through the middle of the darn and out towards the edge of your darning mushroom.

9. Thread your tail threads through your needle and weave them in and out of your stitches to secure in place (see page 35) before trimming.

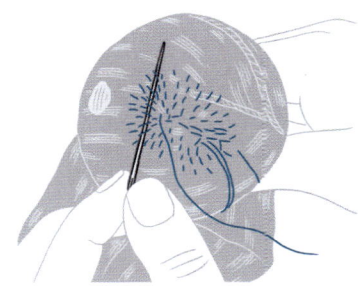

NOTE: The reverse side of your darn will look like a series of firework stitches, and can also be used as the front of your work. For this, just work on the wrong side of the fabric (WS) and finish the tail threads on the wrong side too.

7 *Jackets*

Sportswear and outerwear fabrics are designed to be durable and often waterproof, as well as boasting a whole range of other technical properties. However, exposure to the elements and sports means that they are put through their paces and can face harsh damage.

Because of their varied technical requirements – designed to be reversible, filled with down or similar material for warmth, or coated for water resistance – any holes created with a needle and thread on these kinds of fabrics will leave a permanent mark, and potentially lead to further strain and damage. This means that unpicking any stitches you make is not recommended, so keeping the repairs simple and clean is the best option – in other words, this is where patching comes in! A patch can cover the entire area of damage and be sewn neatly into place using a simple whip stitch.

Puffer jacket

You will need:
A synthetic fabric patch at least 1cm (3⁄8in) bigger all around than the hole; this one was salvaged from an old tent
A fine quilting or embroidery needle
Fine polyester or nylon sewing thread
An iron and an iron-safe fabric scrap

While you can buy specific adhesive patches in various colours, shapes and sizes for technical and sportswear clothing, these won't be a long-term fix. You can see with this puffer jacket that the main hole actually already had a small piece of waterproof tape in place. This has worked well as a quick fix, but was starting to peel away at the edges. If you decide to use adhesive patches, I have found that using circular shapes, or at least eliminating any pointed edges, will help ensure a longer-lasting patch.

My mend:
Wear and tear on a padded jacket, repaired using a patch and whip stitch

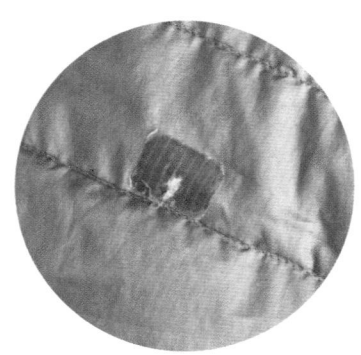

A good tip for stitching into puffer jackets is, where possible, to stitch along existing lines of topstitching so that you aren't adding extra holes (which means extra strain) to the fabric. With this repair, making the patch larger than the hole meant that two sides of the patch could be sewn along existing lines of stitching.

Using pins or basting stitches will create permanent holes in both the fabric patch and the jacket, so with these kinds of repairs it's a case of working very slowly edge by edge while you hold the patch in place, making sure to adjust the patch and jacket as you work so that everything is lying correctly. You can also buy fabric tape that can be used to stick the patch into place before you start sewing.

NOTE: If you ever find yourself with a broken umbrella, tent, sleeping bag or leather bag, I'd recommend holding on to at least a small selection of the fabrics, as they work really well as patches for jackets!

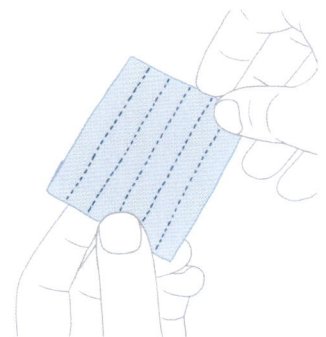
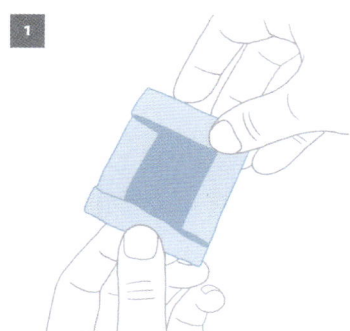

NOTE: To add an element of interest to this otherwise plain black fabric patch, I first used my sewing machine to sew several rows of straight stitching across it. This is a completely optional extra step, but it can help to make the patch feel like a creative embellishment to the jacket, rather than just being stuck on.

1. First you need to fold the edges of the patch under for a clean finish, but don't forget that technical fabrics will be largely made from synthetic fibres and will melt under an iron. To work around this, use your fingers to crease the edges under by about 1cm (⅜in) as best as you can, then cover the patch with a piece of cotton fabric. With the iron on a low heat, and with no steam, press the edges down.

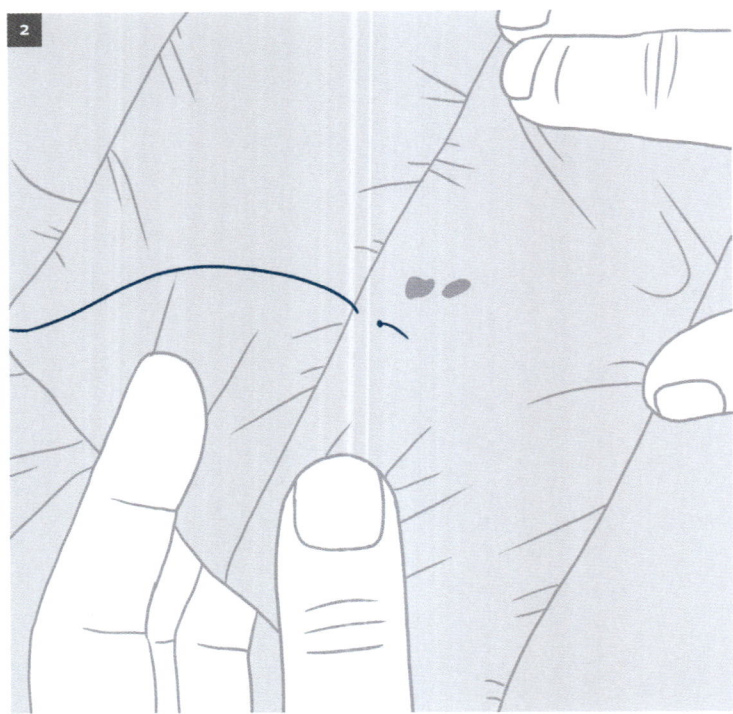

2. Thread your needle and tie a knot in one end of the thread. When you start sewing you can bury this knot between the layers of the patch and jacket.

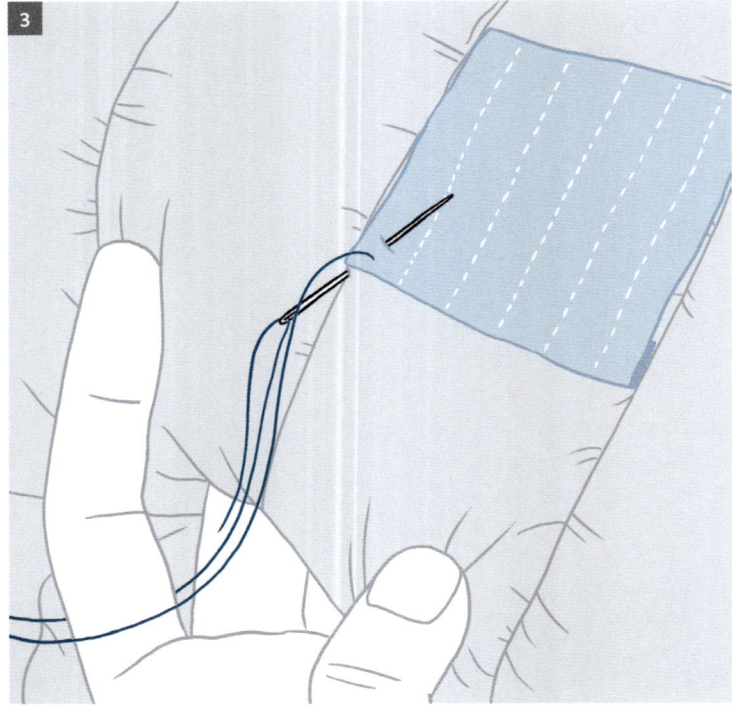

3. Using either a whip stitch or a blanket stitch (see pages 44, 107), begin attaching the patch to the jacket, aiming, if possible, to secure one or two edges of the patch along existing stitches on the jacket.

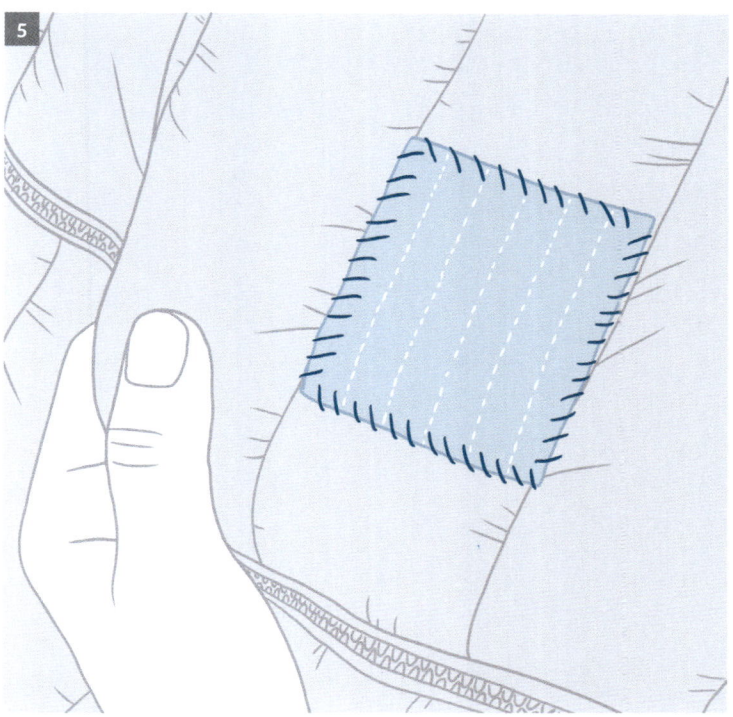

NOTE: As you sew, make sure that you are only stitching through the outer layer of the jacket fabric. With this puffer jacket, if I had sewn through to the lining I would have also sewn through the inside pocket that is used to pack the jacket down in on itself, making it unusable. If you are repairing a jacket that has any kind of down filling, you might find that as you pull your needle through you end up with small feathers or fluff coming through with it. To minimize this I find that holding my thumb down on the exit hole as I pull the thread through means that any feathers caught won't make it up to the top side of the patch.

4. At the end of each edge sewn, stop to check how the patch is lying on top of the fabric and make sure that there are no puckers.

5. When you come back round to the first row of stitching, make one last stitch and tie a knot as close as you can to it, then push your needle through and in between the patch and jacket fabrics and out to the side as far as you can. You can then trim this thread off to finish.

Leather jacket

My mend:
Tears in a leather jacket, repaired using patches

You will need:
Leather scraps
An awl and cutting board
Leather glue
Fine waxed polyester thread
A leather needle
Palm and thumb thimbles

Leather requires extra thought when it comes to repairs, as the same rules about stitch marks apply as to synthetic jackets, and it is much tougher to work through when hand sewing. Leather needles are essential here, as they have a sharp triangular point that allows you to pierce through the leather without ripping it. Thimbles will also make a huge difference when working with leather; I find palm thimbles as well as silicone thumb and fingertip ones are a good combination.

This leather jacket was over 40 years old and covered in various damages, from clean rips and tears and paint stains to a very worn out and peeling collar. I sourced a scrap piece of blue leather from a local leather worker who helped me to pick a piece that was a good match both in weight and texture to the original jacket. After lots of trial and error, I combined lots of different tips and tricks to make patching all of the damage as easy as possible.

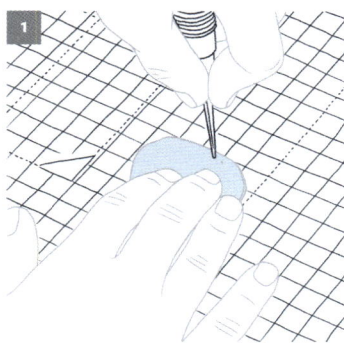

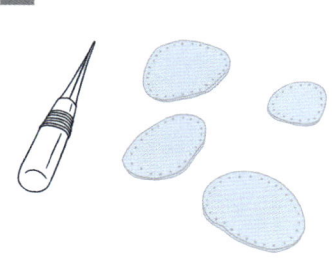

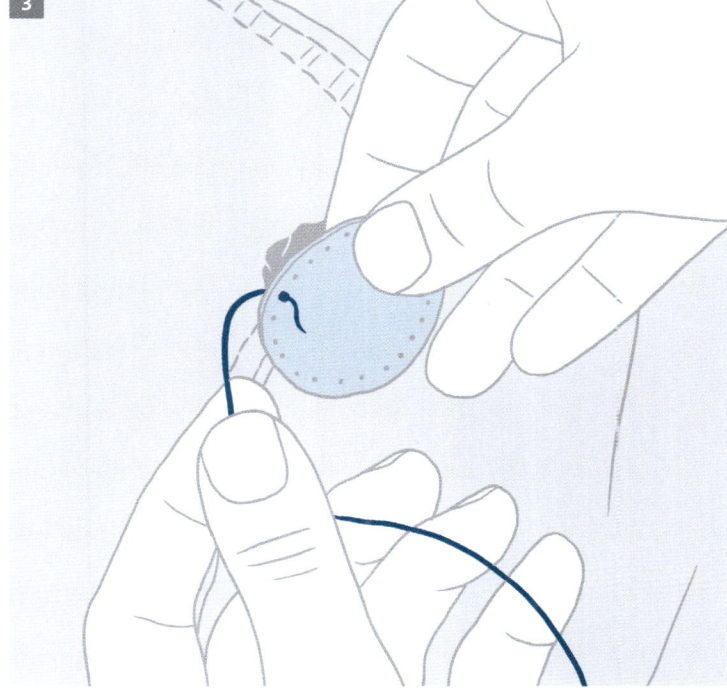

1. First, cut out each patch in an organic circle shape, making sure it is bigger than the hole or tear to cover. A rounded patch helps create a longer-lasting patch, with less worry about pointed edges that can curl and catch.

2. Use a cutting mat and a tailor's awl to pre-punch holes around the edge of the patch for sewing through. I decided on the spacing of these holes as I went, aiming for them to be around 5mm (¼in) apart, but you could always use a fabric marker to mark the holes out before piercing them.

3. Thread up a leather hand-sewing needle with a fine waxed thread and tie a knot in one end. Bring this through one hole on the patch so that the knot ends up on the wrong side of the patch. You can use leather glue (the Bostik one seems to be well known and loved for leather repairs) to secure the patch into place before you start sewing, ensuring the thread knot is sandwiched between the layers. Apply the glue to both the jacket and the patch, making sure not to apply glue at the edges, where the pre-punched holes are, as this will make them much harder to sew through. Once the glue is dry you can begin sewing using the thread that you a ready have attached.

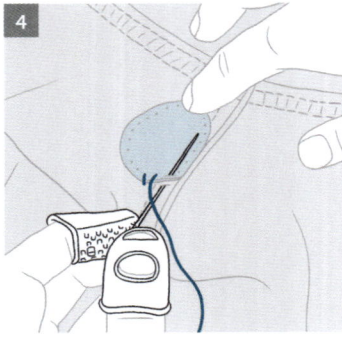

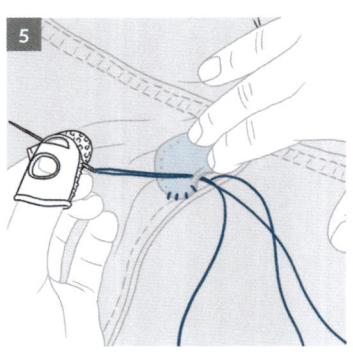

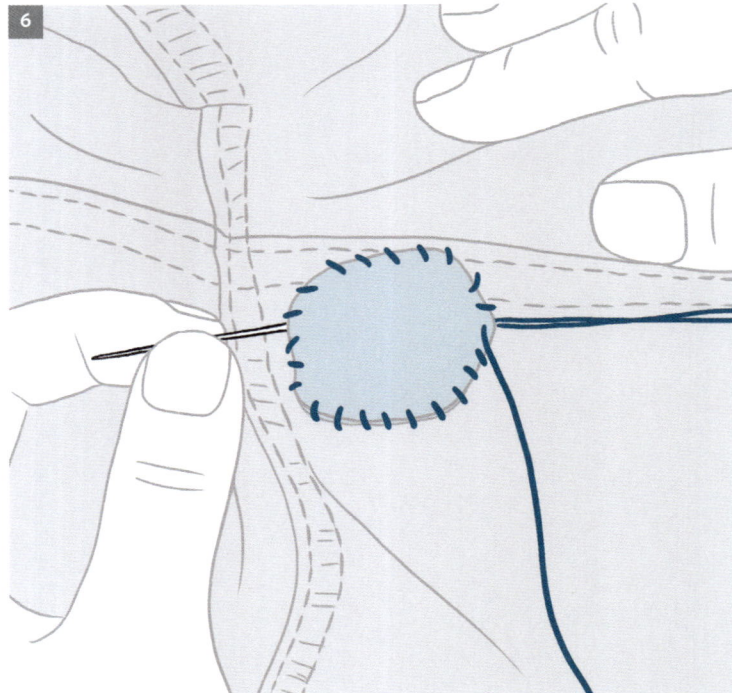

4. Use whip stitch (see page 44) to sew the patch into place, working very slowly when stitching through the leather of the jacket, as it may be fragile in worn areas.

5. Continue sewing whip stitch through the pre-punched holes. Having the holes already in place on the patch makes a huge difference here, as it means your focus can be on sewing through the leather of the jacket.

NOTE: Depending on the garment, you might also have a lining fabric to keep out of the way. If possible, try to move the lining out of the way as much as you can as you are working, and check every few stitches to make sure you haven't sewn through it.

6. Once you have stitched the whole patch into place, push the needle and thread through between the patch and jacket all the way to the other side of the patch, then pull it through.

7. To finish, tie a knot in the thread as close as possible to the edge of the patch and then cut off the excess thread.

8 *Delicate fabrics*

Using what you have learned throughout this book, you can apply these tips and techniques to any other fabrics and types of damage that you come across in your wardrobe.

For example, silk is a super-fine and delicate fibre that is prone to natural degradation from exposure to chemicals and general wear and tear. Silk thread is very soft and is made up of long, continuous fibres that are harvested from the silkworm's cocoon. Often, if several holes have appeared, it's a sign that the fibres may be too far gone to repair, but if you need to repair a snag or small tear then you can choose to darn the area.

If the item has a right and a wrong side, such as silk pyjamas, you can eliminate the need for darning and instead use a very fine iron-on interfacing on the inside (WS) of the clothing to reinforce the tear. This can be used either as an alternative to repairing the damage from the front, or as a first step to add stability to the fabric.

Because of its delicate and fragile nature, a really fine needle will be needed to repair any damage on silk, along with an equally fine silk (or at least cotton/natural) thread. Any holes created with a needle or pins will stay visible, as with waterproof fabrics and leather, so it's best to use fabric clips instead of pins or basting stitches.

Since the scarf repaired in this chapter has no front or back, the repair had to work from both sides, so I chose to create a cross-section of lots of rows of small running stitches around the area, which would look good whichever side of the scarf you look at. These running stitches also helped embed the whole patch into the rest of the scarf once finished.

A FEW POINTS TO KEEP IN MIND

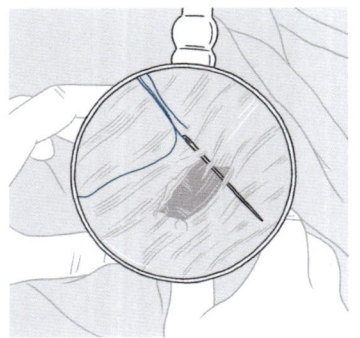
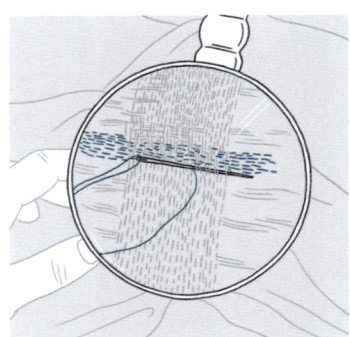

◎ Extra-fine quilting or embroidery needles work well on silk as they are delicate enough to avoid causing further damage to the fabric. If you can match with a silk thread that's great, but here I have used a mix of silk and cotton threads and made sure that the weight was a good match.

◎ I created a fairly subtle visible repair by alternating the colours of the threads every few rows to complement the colours and patterns on the scarf, but of course the colour choices are up to you!

◎ Due to the fine weave of silk, darned patches take a lot longer to build up than they do on socks or knitwear, but the same method still applies, and there's no reason that darning can't be used, as long as you have the time and a light touch to work on it! In this case I didn't create a standard warp and weft foundation to darn from, but used the running stitches to create a foundation of new stitches to work back and forth over to cover the hole and strengthen the area. (I recommend using a magnifying lamp if you have one, as this will really help you to see the structure of the silk fabric and ensure that you can create a fairly even darn on top of it.)

◎ With any delicate or technical fabrics, it's always worth testing out a technique on similar scrap or discarded fabrics if possible. That way you'll get a good feel for the way the fabric moves as you work, as well as getting to grips with any new needles or threads. Alternatively, if you don't have any similar scrap fabrics that are suitable, you can make a few stitches somewhere hidden, or on the inside of the clothing. I do this if I'm ever unsure how a fabric will react to the needle or thread that I want to use; it can really help to see the results before you commit to the whole repair.

FURTHER READING & ACKNOWLEDGEMENTS

There are so many resources that I have learned from over the years, and that have inspired me to keep repairing clothes. Here are a few of my favourite books, podcasts and documentaries if you'd like to learn more about the world of fast fashion.

Read:
Loved Clothes Last by Orsola de Castro
To Die For by Lucy Siegle
Consumed by Aja Barber
The Golden Thread by Kassia St Clair

Listen:
Remember Who Made Them with Venetia La Manna
Fashion Critical with Lucy Siegle and Livia Firth
Conscious Style with Elizabeth Joy
Clotheshorse with Amanda Lee McCarty

Watch:
The True Cost, documentary film by Andrew Morgan
Fashion's Dirty Secrets: Stacey Dooley Investigates, BBC television series
Sashiko Story, a YouTube channel by Atsushi Futatsuya

Writing this book has been a total joy and one that I'll always be grateful for. Thank you, reader, for choosing to pick it up and learn more about visible mending. I hope it inspires you to try out something new to breathe life into a well worn garment and I hope that you'll go on to share the book and these skills with others.

Thank you to Ellie for being such a kind and enthusiastic commissioning editor; for letting me nitpick about the tiniest details that I wanted to be right and for allowing me the creative freedom to just pour myself into the book. To Ben, who really helped to kickstart this whole process into action and totally got what I wanted the book to be. To Faye, Laura and the rest of the team at Ilex and to Kim who brought the book to life with her incredible photography, I'm so grateful to all of you!

To the amazing visible mending community (especially on Instagram) who constantly inspire me and spur me on to keep mending and to everyone who has supported my shop and attended workshops with me over the last few years.

To everyone who lent their clothes to me for the book, thank you for trusting me to repair them for you. I hope that you love the repairs and that all of these garments can be loved and worn for many more years.

To my friends who have supported me, been excited with me, who have let me experiment with mending techniques on their clothes over the years and who have always embraced the textiles geek in me and made me feel that what I'm doing matters.

A huge thank you and so much love to my Mum and awesome family, and especially to my little sister and best friend Tia – thank you for being my biggest cheerleader and for the endless support you have given me throughout this process. Also to my nieces and nephews, who are always at the front of my mind when I'm working on these small stitches that I hope will – even if in a small way – help to create a kinder and greener world for them to grow up in.

And finally, this book never would have seen the light of day if it wasn't for my partner, Jason. He has believed in me and pushed me to be the best version of myself since we met as teenagers and I am so grateful to him for that. For all the hours on dog walks or cooking together while pondering chapter ideas, and for the weekends you gave up to help me create a makeshift photography studio in the attic, thank you.